God b

Love and Prayers

Maryanne Raphael

Mother Teresa,

Called to Love

Mother Teresa
an original watercolor impression by J.R. Roosenberg

Mother Teresa, Called to Love

by Maryanne Raphael

Writer's World (*International Press*)
Waverly, Ohio

Mother Teresa, Called to Love.

Grateful acknowledgement to:

Dr. Anita Figueredo, Mildred Strohm, Jacqueline de Decker, Zulema Hokanson for supplying and giving permission to use the photographs contained within.
J.R. Roosenberg for donating her drawings.
Millie Crawford for her painting of Mother Teresa.

Requests for information or permission to make copies of any part of the work should be made to:

The Editor & Publisher,
Writer's World (*International Press*),
334 Morningside Drive, Waverly, Ohio 45690, USA.
E-mail: writers_world@yahoo.com
Website: www.writersworldinternational.com

Raphael, Maryanne.
Mother Teresa, Called to Love/Maryanne Raphael.
ISBN 0-9679865-0-8
LCCN 00-101961

Contents Page

Preface

Maryanne Raphael's book about Mother Teresa and the Missionaries of Charity, is an accurate, clearly written, unfurbished biography which all will find inspiring and instructive. It manages to convey the spirit of Mother and the Missionaries of Charity in a manner which all who know them will recognize as authentic, and all who have not had that privilege will want to become acquainted and learn from them.

The book is easy to read and very informative. I recommend it to all readers, especially young ones, whether they have been devoted followers of Mother Teresa or have not known her except as a person often written about by the press. All will find inspiration in it. *Mother Teresa, Called to Love* is a work of love by the author, and it shows.

—Anita V. Figueredo, M.D., Member of the Board of Trustees of the University of San Diego, Co-Worker and longtime friend of Mother Teresa

Acknowledgements

I wish to thank Mother Teresa for the letter of permission which allowed me access to her Missionaries of Charity, Co-Workers and friends. I thank all of them for their willing cooperation: Jacqueline de Decker, International Link of the Sick and Suffering Co-Workers; Ann Blaikie, International Link of the Co-Workers; Vi Collins, National Link of the Co-Workers; Michael Gomes, Mother Teresa's friend and first landlord in whose "upper room" she began the Missionaries of Charity; Ed and Dorothy Baroch, Youth Link of the Co-Workers of Mother Teresa; Dr. Anita Figueredo, Mother's friend and longtime Co-Worker; Lillian Miceli-Farrugia, International Youth Link; the Missionaries of Charity, and the many Co-Workers who helped: Zulema Hokanson and her family, Kyle, Melissa and Jeffry; Lupe Rios, Irene Nicolai, Nancy Morgan, Susanna Miranda, and Phyllis Cooper; Alice Volpe.

Co-Worker Margaret Delaney, who helped me finish the book when I felt overwhelmed; Grace Kessler, a Co-Worker who put the entire book on the computer before I learned how to use one; Ann Liddell, author and editor, who devoted many hours to editing the final version of the book.

Don Johnson and Craig Burgess, who rescued my computer more than once; Dorothy Johnson, who rescued me from many physical problems so I could concentrate on the book; the Librarians at Parker Ranch on the Big Island of Hawaii, at Waverly, Ohio, Carlsbad, California and Seattle, Washington, who helped me with my research far beyond the call of duty.

My son Raphael Raphael whose constant support, loving encouragement, editorial feedback and research help made the task lighter; his wife Ginger for her sunshine and sparkling love; Wendy Heckett and her advanced creative writing class; the Phoenix Poets of Shawnee University; Helen Kolodny, Andrea Glass, Louise Goodman, J.R. Roosenberg and all the members of the Grape Group Writers for their enthusiasm, excellent critique and helpful suggestions.

Little Karen from San Rafael who sent me her information on Mother Teresa's childhood; Val Michaels for sharing his personal experiences growing up in Yugoslavia; Joan Taylor for her faithful friendship and the use of her computer; Ethel Andrade, Katya De La Metier, Allison and Eli Boroda, Brenda and Tom Ray, Claudia Suen, Carol Andrus, Cynthia Hassan, Dee Markwood, Dr. Eve Jones, Elizabeth Baumgarten, Elizabeth James, Robert and Carolyn Gover, Leilani Jiminez, J'Nelle Gement, Steve Holland, Jan and Tom Unger, Patti Graf, Jim Henry, Betty Jo and Bill Gildow, Pepper Baxter, Pat Rhone, Rose Moore, Gabriella Whitehead,

Thelma Hayes for their constant support; St. Anthony's small church group for inspiration; Jeni Wolf for her editing and friendship; Julia Uz, Alex and Jon Wolf.

Bob Stahl, Joyce Grubbe, Chelsea, Kara Trent and Rae Ann Rasmussen for making it possible for me to continue working on my book during my visit to Seattle; Millie Crawford for painting the beautiful portrait of Mother Teresa especially for the book.

My family in Ohio, Doris Patterson, Doctor Dodo, Fred, Susie, Frankie, Kathy, Felix, Butch, Barb, Nancy, Steve, Tom, Penny, Jim, Sherry, Mike, and Marion for being there for me.

And I wish to thank all of you who purchased the book. Mother Teresa asked me to pray that *Called to Love* will glorify God and bring many souls to Him.

Thank you for helping me pray.

—Maryanne Raphael

What Mother Teresa Taught Me About Love

When Mother Teresa of Calcutta won the Nobel Peace Prize in 1979, I was teaching the Geography and History of India at St. Joseph's high school in Hawaii. A free-lance writer, I was substitute teaching to supplement my writing income. I believe this was the first step in a predestined journey that brought me into the exciting, demanding world of Mother Teresa.

I brought books about Mother Teresa to class and my students asked to borrow them. Seeing how she appealed to teenagers, I decided to write a book about her especially for young adults.

I researched books, articles and videos and contacted every name I came across in my reading that had a connection with Mother Teresa; almost every one answered. When I tried to reach Mother Teresa's Co-Workers in Hawaii, I was given names and addresses and asked to organize a group. Later I learned this is the way the Co-Workers work, if you ask for something worthwhile that doesn't exist, you are asked to create it. The only address on the Big Island, where I lived, was in Kona, about one hundred miles away. I decided to look for other Co-Workers and to get together with them at the first opportunity.

Before we could meet, my sister Susie called to say our brother John was dying. Three hours later, Raphael, my twelve-year-old son, and I were on the way to Ohio. I calmed myself by reading Mother's words about "beautiful deaths," descriptions of people who had died in her homes "with a ticket to St. Peter," and her great faith that death is simply going home to God.

We arrived in time to tell John good-bye. It was the first death in our immediate family and brought the remaining nine brothers and sisters closer together. Instead of returning to Hawaii, Raphael and I remained with our Ohio family. I joined Mother Teresa's Co-Workers, even though the nearest Missionaries of Charity were in Jenkins, Kentucky, and the nearest Co-Workers were in Cleveland, all hundreds of miles away. I went to Cleveland to meet Ann Blaikie, the official founder of the International Co-Workers. I will never forget her words: "I was coordinating an International Co-Worker's Conference in Rome where Mother Teresa was speaking. Just as I was leaving my house, my neighbor arrived. 'My sister just died,' she said, 'and I'm all alone.' I called Rome to say I couldn't make the conference, and spent the weekend consoling my neighbor. I knew that was what Mother Teresa would want me to do. Mother always says our love and caring must begin at home."

After our meeting, I left Ohio for New York City to write a book about Akita dogs. I also volunteered as a Vista Worker, the domestic version of the Peace Corps, and worked with the Sisters of St. Joseph at the Center for Family Life, helping troubled teenagers.

One day I received a post card from a friend in Hawaii. It said: "You have a good friend in the Bronx. My friend, Sister Frances [I have changed her name here], and I were both engaged to be married when she fell in love with Jesus. She became one of Mother Teresa's nuns caring for the dying. Find her, tell her you and Raphael are our adopted family and she will welcome you with open arms." Right away I wrote a letter to Sister Frances. Since I did not have her official address I wrote to: "Sister Frances, Missionary of Charity Working with Mother Teresa in the Bronx." I put the envelope in the mail, not really expecting an answer, and forgot about it.

Two months later I received a phone call. "Hello, this is Sister Frances. I got your post card even though I no longer live in New York. I am here right now and would like you to come this weekend when I make my vows. Mother Teresa will be there."

That was in June 1982. On the morning of the ceremony, Raphael and I took the train uptown to the Bronx. When we got out of the subway, the scenery looked like a war zone. One building after another had been demolished for future construction. St. Rita's church was large and a huge crowd had gathered to catch a glimpse of Mother Teresa. We attended a Mass where eight Sisters took their vows. When Mother Teresa walked up to the altar, I was astonished to see how short she was, and yet her energy was so powerful she may as well have been eight feet tall. Her smile and her loving eyes blessed each one of us individually, even from afar. She told little anecdotes about how beautiful the poor are. "I took some rice to a large Muslim family. Before they took a bite, the mother carefully divided the food and took half to her Hindu neighbors. When she returned she said, 'They are hungry too, Mother.'"

I was to hear Mother Teresa tell that same story many times, but it always sounded fresh and touching. It meant so much to her. She was comfortable with English but had a strong Indian accent. Her voice was soft yet she mesmerized her audience. Each person felt she was confiding in them alone. Mother always spoke of Jesus. She saw Him in the Blessed Sacrament, the poor, the dying, in everyone, and her all-consuming love touched us deeply.

After Mass, everyone lined up to shake Mother's hand. "God bless you," she told each of us. Then there was a reception for the new Sisters and their families. Raphael and I were Sister Frances' "family." When I told Sister Frances I was writing a book about Mother Teresa for young adults, she rushed me over to Mother.

Mother reached out her hand, shook mine, smiled and said, "God Bless you." I told her I was working with young Puerto Rican gang members. "They read biographies of musicians, famous athletes, movie stars, or politicians," I said, "and many of those people had lived very sad, even tragic lives. I want to write books about people who have lived joyful, meaningful lives. That's why I want to write about you, Mother Teresa."

"Write about the work," she said.

I told her that my favorite books when I was young were about famous people when they were children. Each became my playmate because they remained a child until the last chapter. At the end of the book, I was proud of my friend's accomplishments when they grew up.

I asked, "Mother, would you tell me a little about your childhood?"

"Write about the work," Mother said again with a big smile.

Our conversation was interrupted many times. Everyone was eager to speak with Mother Teresa and kept coming to her with questions, requests or statements of love and respect. They all said, "It's such a blessing to meet you, Mother." Mother gave each of them her warm, loving smile.

Sister Frances was anxious for me to meet the other nuns. She told them about my book. Each Sister brought me back to Mother and once more Mother squeezed my hand, smiled, and we resumed our conversation. I continued my questions, and each time Mother replied, "Write about the work." When I asked, "Mother, what was your favorite color when you were a child?" she reached for my hand, and that same warm smile brightened her face. "Please," she said, "don't write about me."

"But Mother, youth need to read about people who have found their path."

Mother finally said, "We'll see."

After that day, I had a new focus for my book, "the work." My research led me to Michael Gomes, the man in whose upper room Mother Teresa first began her Missionaries of Charity. I was overjoyed when I received a letter from him, with a return address of 14 Creek Lane, Calcutta, the locale now famous in Mother's history. Michael continues to write to me today. His letters are always informative, inspiring and supportive.

Not long after we met Mother Teresa, our friends Fred and Taia Chard invited Raphael and me to return to Hawaii and live with them. We flew to California and stopped over in San Rafael, where we visited a friend. Raphael and I went to Mass at the old mission and afterwards visited the little book shop. A young girl walked up to me and asked, "Have you seen any books about St. Claire?"

I pointed to an entire shelf.

"Have you seen any books about Mother Teresa?" I asked.

"Yes, there against the wall," she said. "You know, I met Mother Teresa last month when she opened a house in San Francisco. I went to the Press Conference because I write for my school newspaper. Mother Teresa gave me some papers about when she was a little girl."

"Could I see the papers?" I asked excitedly.

"My priest is reading them," she said. "When I get them back from him, I'll send them to you."

I gave her my Hawaiian address but I never expected to hear from her. Two months later, settled in Hawaii, I received a package from San Rafael. The young girl, whose name was Karen, had kept her word. I received the information about Mother's childhood that I had been unable to find elsewhere. I saw this as another miracle. I was convinced Karen was an angel and this was a sign that God wanted me to know about Mother's childhood.

I joined a Catholic Women's Movement and Meditation Group. We met once a month at a different location each time. One month I took the bus around the island and got off at a convent where I thought the group was meeting. A nun told me, "You're at the wrong place. The women are meeting at the next convent about five miles down the road."

"I came on the bus," I said, "By the time I walk there the group will be finished."

"I have to go over there anyway to deliver some papers," the nun said. "I'll take you now."

When we got in the car, the Sister told me she had recently attended the Third World Conference on Women in Mexico. She had worked with Mother Teresa on Natural Birth Control! Another miracle! I interviewed her. Her information was an invaluable addition to my research. What began as a chance meeting led me to another angel.

A few months later, I took a trip to New York where I made arrangements to work in the soup kitchen run by Mother's Missionaries of Charity. It was located in the same building on 145th street in the East Bronx that Raphael and I had visited before. I was staying with friends on the Lower East Side. To arrive at 6:00 a.m. for Mass, I had to leave home at 4:30 a.m. It was still dark and I was alone on the New York subway. I thought about how the Sisters usually traveled by two's and wished I had a partner. I looked at my watch when I came out of the subway. It was 5:30 a.m. Strange shadows and crumbling ruins looked menacing as I walked down the deserted street. From behind a hand touched my arm. I was very frightened. A man's voice asked, "Are you lost, lady?" I was relieved when I turned and looked into the kind face of a small, elderly, dark man. I said, "I'm looking for Mother Teresa's Missionaries of Charity." He told me his name was Angel Rafael Rodriguez and he was delivering newspapers in the neighborhood. He said proudly, "I know Mother Teresa's Sisters well. I will take you there when I finish my route." Angel Rodriguez and I finished his rounds. He had a smile and a word for everyone which they returned in kind. He walked me to the convent and waited until the Sisters answered the door. After helping the Sisters with their clothing project and soup kitchen, I gave them a copy of the first three chapters of my book.

One month later, back home in Hawaii, I received a letter saying: "Mother Teresa has given you permission to write and publish a book about her work." It looked like angels had been working for me again.

Another angel in my life was Jacqueline de Decker, the Link for the Sick and Suffering Co-Workers—people who can't work with Mother and her Sisters because of their illnesses, but can offer their prayers and sufferings for the work. My first letter to Jacqueline was in French, but she insisted I write her in English because I spelled God "Dieux," which means more than one God. "I hope you aren't writing your book in French," she joked.

My work on the book slowed down when, in early 1990, I moved to Southern California and my new doctor sent me for a CT scan. The scan showed a life-threatening tumor in my head.

I wrote to Jacqueline asking to be a sick and suffering Co-Worker. Whenever I felt sick, I found it hard to pray even though I felt an urgent need for prayers. So, while I could make a conscious decision, I wanted to offer all my pain and discomfort to the Lord. Jacqueline de Decker's reply made me feel better about my operation. Being a Sick and Suffering Co-Worker made me feel closer to Jesus and less afraid.

The day I got my CT scan results I was scheduled to spend the night in Encinitas at Bethlehem Lutheren Church as part of our Co-Worker's program to shelter the homeless. I called my friend Irene, another Co-Worker, asking her to relieve me. She believed in tough love and let me have it: "Don't tell me you're going to desert the homeless just because you need an operation at some future date! I'm sorry you're sick and I will pray for you every day. But your comfortable bed at home isn't going to be any better for you than a sleeping bag in the basement. In the church you will be too busy and have too many immediate problems to worry about your own. I will make your phone calls and tell everyone what food to bring. Get some rest so you will be ready to work tonight."

I did spend the night with the homeless in the church basement which was the best thing I could have done. It set the pattern for me to continue my life as close to normal as possible while I prepared for the brain surgery. And as Mother Teresa said, the poor have so much to teach us. That night, a couple from San Salvador brought in a one-year-old baby who was in immediate danger of dying from pneumonia. Their problem soon made me forget mine.

Following Mother's example, I turned to prayer, Mass, the Eucharist, Rosaries and the Bible for healing. I had everyone I knew praying for me. One day when I was reading how Jesus the Good Shepherd would leave ninety-nine good sheep to look for a lost sheep, I thought of my friend Mona, who claimed to be an atheist. I wrote asking for her prayers: "I know you don't believe in God, but you believe in me and I believe in God. I am having a life-threatening operation and I feel that God longs for atheists' prayers. So your prayers could be very helpful."

In her reply, Mona wrote: "Your letter moved me. I shared it with the Atheists Club and invited any of them to stay afterwards and pray for you. Every single member stayed. Some of us prayed for the first time. Let us know how you make out."

I was thinking about Mona's words when the surgeon explained to me that my head would have to be shaved. This was an obstacle that I hadn't considered. I thought about my friend Janet, who had died of cancer. During her last months she refused to leave the house because her wigs kept sliding off her smooth, bald head. I did not want to give up my hair. For days I cried and complained to my friends. I was bitter.

My son Raphael brought me some photos and videos of glamorous women with bald heads. "See, Maryanne," he said. "They have style. These women cut off their hair because they feel you don't need hair to be beautiful. Beauty comes from within."

I was not yet ready to acknowledge his words of comfort. Was it my pride that refused to accept the baldness? Then I read how Mother Teresa and her nuns cut off their beautiful hair to become Missionaries of Charity.

"Give Jesus anything He asks and take anything He gives with a smile," Mother advised us. And her example showed us how. Mother's words helped me to put aside my vanity and accept the inevitable. The evening before my operation, my friend Phyllis, a hair dresser, cut and arranged my hair in different styles. We photographed each one. She promised to recreate my favorite when my hair returned.

The operation lasted nine and one-half hours and the doctors expected me to spend several weeks in the hospital. I was out of intensive care in one night and home after five days.

When they took off the bandages and removed the stitches there was almost no scar. Every doctor who saw me after the operation said, "That was really a miracle!"

I went to Ohio to visit my family. They too rejoiced in the "miracle." One day when we were all gathered at my sister Kathy's house, my nine-year-old niece Courtney shouted, "Your Mother Teresa is famous!" "Yes, I know. She won the Nobel Peace Prize!"

"It's better than that," Courtney said. "She's on MTV with Michael Jackson!" She called me to the television set to watch a video of Michael singing about the "man in the mirror" while movie clips were shown, among them Mother Teresa in Africa.

After I recuperated, I returned to San Diego and watched Mother Teresa receive an honorary doctorate at the University of San Diego. Maureen O'Conner, the Mayor of San Diego, gave Mother the key to the city and asked, "Why would she want the key to any city when she has the key to Heaven?"

During the entire preliminary session Mother sat on the stage saying her Rosary. As they introduced her, describing her many achievements, Mother never stopped praying.

"And here she is: Mother Teresa!"

Mother went on fingering her beads.

"Mother Teresa of Calcutta!"

The crowd applauded and everyone stood up. Mother continued praying her Rosary.

Finally someone walked over to her. "Mother, it's your turn to talk now."

Mother put away her Rosary, walked up to the mike and began speaking to us with the same intensity and concentration she had put into her prayers. "When Our Lady learned she was going to give birth to Jesus, she went in haste to tell her cousin Elizabeth the good news, and to help Elizabeth celebrate her own news that she was to give birth to John the Baptist. And I think we must ask ourselves: Do we go in haste to take Jesus to the poor?" Her small clear voice captured the attention of everyone in the audience.

Mother got our attention in another way. On a sweltering August night in the border town of Tijuana, a group of us Co-Workers were camping in the Missionaries of Charity seminary when the bare light bulb suddenly flashed and went out.

"Hey, who turned out the light?"

Mother's voice called back, "It is late and tomorrow is a busy day! And we mustn't waste money meant for the poor on electricity!" None of us could believe that the soft but stern voice with the Bengali accent belonged to Mother Teresa.

Mother Teresa switched the light back on, waited a few minutes for us to settle into our sleeping bags, then shut the light off for the night. "God bless you," Mother Teresa said into the blackness.

Now whenever I leave the lights on too long, I am reminded of Mother coming to turn them off.

The next morning, we attended the Ordination of one of Mother Teresa's Missionaries of Charity Brothers. Mother gave a short talk: "God took on a little body, such a little body, and we find it so hard to become little. But Jesus tells us that unless you become like little children, you shall not enter the Kingdom of God."

After the Ordination, we Co-Workers waited outside the building to talk with Mother Teresa. Inside, Mother met with her nuns. Someone opened the window next to where I stood. It was as though I had been invited to share Mother's private moment with her Sisters. Every time Mother said something the Sisters laughed with joy. There was something so mystical about Mother's voice and the nuns' laughter that I found myself feeling high. It felt like Mother was speaking to my heart rather than my mind.

I remember thinking, "They remind me of Zen Koans, puzzles that Buddhist masters use to teach their students, sentences like 'What is the sound of one hand clapping?'"

But Mother offered no puzzles. She was expressing her joy at seeing her Sisters. I understood, or thought I understood, every word Mother said. But immediately afterwards as the Sisters laughed I forgot everything and my mind was a complete blissful blank.

My eyes were focused on the door to the building. At any moment someone would invite us to join Mother.

I felt someone squeeze my hand. I looked around but didn't see anyone. Then I glanced down and there was Mother Teresa. Her head barely reached my chest. The skin of her hand was rough like a laborer's, but her energy was tender and uplifting. Warmth flooded my body. I knew she was praying for me. I thought, "This is like holding hands with Jesus." Never before had I felt such happiness, a deep peace with joyful excitement. Kissing a Miraculous medal, Mother lovingly put it in my hand, patted my fist and walked away. I could not believe this was real.

A huge monk came out of the building and called, "Please come back inside, Mother. It isn't safe out here!" He tried to hold onto her, but she squirmed out of his hands and seemed to dive into the crowd, continuing to kiss medals and pass them out.

The memories of the precious days I spent with Mother Teresa in the Bronx, San Diego and Tijuana will always remain in my mind.

Once we had a meeting at Dr. Anita Figueredo's house and a Co-Worker offered a washer and dryer to the Sisters in Tijuana. We found a truck and when we arrived, Mother said, "No thank you. The Sisters don't need this." So we prayed about it. My friend Lupe and I asked God to show us what to do with the washer and dryer. Many Mexican people kept asking about it, but most of them did not have water or electricity. Finally a lady with five children who had water and electricity asked for the washer and dryer. We decided the Holy Spirit wanted her to have it. Mother said, "Give it to the person who needs it most. We don't need it." The poor lady was so happy. We knew God intended the machine for her family and had used us as His instruments.

Mother Teresa sent me a beautiful letter for my fiftieth birthday: "I will be praying for you on your birthday and I wish you fifty more years to serve the Lord in your neighbor and in God's beloved poor." When I showed the letter to my friend Ann, she asked me, "What was Mother Teresa really like? Was she as serious as she appears in photos?" That question shocked me because in my photos Mother is happy. I remember her laughing or smiling most of the time. Having a good sense of humor is one of the most important requirements for being a Missionary of Charity. "The poor have enough sorrow of their own," Mother would say. "We must bring them joy."

Ann also asked me how working with Mother Teresa changed my life. Completely. I went from a lukewarm cradle Catholic to a daily communicant with a radical faith in My Father Who Owns the Sky. Mother Teresa said we should never worry about money. "God gives us enough money for anything He wants us to do." Mother took care of thousands of people and never worried about anything. She turned all her would-be worries over to God.

At first I thought, "That's fine for you, Mother Teresa. You're a saint. Of course, God will take care of you. But I'm a single parent with health problems. I have to look out for my son and myself." After spending time with Mother Teresa, I have learned that God is always there for Raphael and me with the same tender love He showed Mother.

In 1992, when Mother had a heart attack brought on by pneumonia, she was admitted to Scripps Hospital in La Jolla, California. She stayed in the hospital for a long time. Dr. Anita Figueredo, Link for the Co-Workers in San Diego, and Dr. Patricia Aubnel looked after her. Some of us went to the hospital to see how Mother was doing. The doctors told us that she was critical. We all went into the chapel and prayed. After Mother Teresa was released from the hospital, she went to spend Christmas in the children's home in El Florido, Mexico, about twenty miles south of Tijuana. We were very worried about Mother since we went to the children's home on a regular basis and knew the situation—the weather was cold and there was no heat in the home. There was no running water, very limited amounts of drinking water, the children had lots of colds and fevers and we were afraid they would give Mother a children's disease, if she didn't freeze to death first.

We could understand why Mother would want to go there because of the smiles on the faces of the nuns and the children, the way the children would reach out and run up to you for hugs. As she had survived health threats from around the world, Mother survived the Mexican Children's Home and had a joyful Christmas.

Mother sent me a note thanking me for my prayers. She wrote:

"Dear Maryanne, With deep appreciation I thank you for remembering me in your prayers. My gratitude will be my prayer for you that you may become humble like Mary so as to become more and more like Jesus. Together, let us thank God for all His tender love and care. He has been so good to me. The care that I received while in the hospital has been something great and beautiful. I am spoiled. Now that I have left the hospital and am feeling better, I ask you to pray much for China. We have been invited to bring Jesus to the people there who are hungering so much for God. Continue to pray for me and my Sisters that we may not spoil God's work. Always be one heart full of love in the hearts of Jesus and Mary. God bless you, M. Teresa M.C."

If any one ever deserved to be spoiled, it was Mother Teresa of Calcutta.

When she left Tijuana and southern California, Mother went to Albania for the first time and opened a house in Tirana where her own mother and sister had died.

I remained in southern California praying with the Co-Workers, helping out at the soup kitchen in Tijuana, bringing clothes and holding the babies in the orphanage in El Florido. I continued working on my book and attending writers' workshops.

In August 1997, my friend and Co-Worker Irene invited me to go home with her to South Africa to see her father, who was very ill. One of the first things we did in Cape Town was to make arrangements to visit the Missionaries of Charity. Early Sunday morning, August 31, 1997, Mother's friend Princess Diana was killed in an automobile accident in Paris. Mother Teresa made a public statement: "She was in love with the poor, anxious to do something for them; that is why we were so close. All the Sisters and I are praying for her and all the members of the family, may they know God's speed and peace and comfort in this moment."

Five days later, on the evening of September 5, 1997, Irene's father and I were watching a program about the death of Princess Diana when a special bulletin announced that Mother Teresa had just died. The most difficult part of watching Diana's funeral for me was to watch and hear the choir sing Mother Teresa's favorite prayer, "St. Francis' Prayer for Peace," which the Co-Workers are asked to say each day. It begins, "Lord, make me a channel of Thy peace; that where there is hatred, I may bring love . . ." and ends, "Lord, grant that I may seek rather to comfort than to be comforted, to understand than to be understood; to love rather than to be loved; for it is by forgetting self that one finds; it is forgiving that one is forgiven; it is by dying that one awakens to eternal life."

I cried for Mother and for Diana. Not really for them, but for us who had lost them. It seemed so strange that Mother Teresa and Princess Diana, who loved and admired one another, should both die within such a short time.

When Irene and I went to the bakery the next day, everyone was talking about Mother Teresa's death. A young girl who worked there said, "I met Mother Teresa once in the airport. She held my hand and smiled at me. I will never forget her smile. Or the way I felt when I was with her. I'm so blessed!" I knew what she meant.

The next day the Sisters called to say they had been invited to Parliament. The National Assembly passed a resolution expressing its sorrow at the death of Mother Teresa, paying tribute to her and offering its condolences. The Sisters asked us to meet them at the Archbishop's home when they left Parliament. They invited us to go home with them. Father Curran, their pastor, drove us there. As we traveled into the countryside outside of Cape Town, we celebrated Mother's heavenly joy and mourned our earthy loss, trying to focus on the joy, but each of us found tears rolling down our faces.

For a short time in the history of eternity an angel touched the earth. I was blessed to spend precious days with her. I feel a little more at home, a little better for having shared the world with a saint.

Mother Teresa inspired me to love my own family, my neighborhood, my town passionately. Then I could truly love the world. She convinced me My Father Who Owns the Sky loves me with an unconditional love and will give me anything I need.

She taught me to love Jesus in all I meet, to smile at Him in His most distressing disguise when I see Him in a person who is angry, boring or irritating. She taught me to be ready to forgive at all times, for how could I stay angry at Jesus no matter

His disguise?

Mother often spoke of how perfect love cast out fear and she helped me conquer my fear of death, to see death as the way home. When my own father was dying, I was able to comfort him during his last night and share his last moments.

Her love for life was an "uncut quilt." She taught me to love life wherever I found it, in an unborn child, a leper, a condemned serial killer, someone with AIDS, a dying person. She often ended her talks with: "It's not how much we do, but how much love we put into it." My goal is to put some of Mother's all-consuming love into everything I do.

Mother once said, "If you don't know any poor people, how do you know their needs?"

I had always felt writing was my mission and felt no compulsion to do any other service. What Mother taught me was that if I was to write about "her work," I would have to get in there and get my hands dirty. I became an active Co-Worker. I helped in soup kitchens, changed diapers and fed babies in children's shelters, cared for and comforted the elderly sick and poor.

Mother taught me that without love, there can be no writing. Without love, there is no passion and no compassion. Without love, there is no meaning.

Maryanne Raphael with Mother Teresa's nuns in South Africa.

"Thousands die every year," the priest said. "Hundreds of thousands live and die in the streets of Calcutta never having had a home."

Agnes Bojaxhiu, now known to the world as Mother Teresa, heard these words when she was only twelve years old. She could see the beautiful Himalayan Mountains of which he spoke, hear the babies crying because they were hungry, and feel the poor half-naked Indian people's pain as they slept on wet sidewalks because they had no home.

That day, Agnes heard God's voice.

Skopje

At the turn of the 20th century, Agnes Bojaxhiu's parents, two young Albanians, very much in love, married in the town of Prizen in Serbia. Dranafile ("Drana") Bernai was gentle but very strong, while Nikola Bojaxhiu was a handsome young man devoted to the movement for an independent Albania. Although most Albanians were Muslims or Orthodox Jews, both Drana and Nikola came from many generations of devout Roman Catholics whose lives centered around the activities and beliefs of their church.

After their wedding, Drana and Nikola settled in Skopje, Macedonia, a small mountain town in what was, in those days, a part of the Turkish Ottoman Empire. Skopje was a town where East met West, where Muslims, Christians, and Jews lived together in relative peace. Nikola and an Italian friend began a successful construction business; soon Nikola owned several houses and was a member of the Skopje Town Council.

A daughter, Aga, was born in 1905, and three years later a son, Lazar, named for Nikola's father. Then two daughters died shortly after birth. Finally on August 26, 1910, baby Agnes Gonxha was born. An infant with round cheeks and sparkling eyes, she would one day be known to the world as Mother Teresa of Calcutta, founder of the Missionaries of Charity, and winner of the Nobel Peace Prize.

Although a lively, mischievous tomboy with an infectious sense of humor, from an early age Agnes was devoted to her family and to her church. She learned from her parents to trust God's will and, as a young child, she was diligent in her attempts to live a life that reflected this belief.

Late one afternoon, nine-year-old Agnes skipped along a cobblestone street in the heart of Skopje's business district, swinging her school books. She peered eagerly into the windows of the small shops. It was a hot summer day and beads of perspiration shone on her forehead as she looked up at the clear blue, cloudless sky.

She was curious about everything, from the goings-on in the shops to the peaceful shepherds grazing their sheep on the nearby mountains. She left the narrow winding street and was soon moving past the gypsy quarter, smiling at the peasants in their thick homespun black tops and baggy, bright colored pantaloons.

Everywhere there were Turks in their red Fez hats. The year was 1919, and Skopje, dominated by a huge graceful mosque and a 16th century fortress built by the Byzantines, was Agnes' whole world.

Nearing her middle-class home, she heard the sound of children's laughter and hastened to join the fun. Her fourteen-year-old sister, Aga, and her eleven-year-old brother, Lazar, were sitting on the living room sofa whispering jokes to one another and giggling. Agnes rushed into the room, hastily greeted her sedate mother, and joined the others. Seated in a rocking chair at the far corner of the room, Drana glanced first at the children and then at the large clock on the wall. As she darned their socks, their mother tried to ignore the steadily rising crescendo of children's voices. Agnes soon had her brother helpless with laughter collapsing on the living room rug. Quickly and without a change of expression, Drana stood up, lay her sewing on the table and left the room. Suddenly the entire house went dark. The laughter stopped.

"What happened?" the children cried in unison.

"There is no need to waste light on such foolishness," their mother's voice cut through the darkness. It was neither stern nor playful, merely matter-of-fact and characteristically efficient.

"Idleness is a sin. Let every act be worthy in the sight of God. Now, I am sure you children can find something constructive to do. Clean your rooms, and Aga, I can use some help in the kitchen."

Immediately, the main switch was thrown and the quieted children filed dutifully to their tasks with subdued faces as the lights reappeared. Their mother again glanced at the clock on the wall and rushed to change her dress and brush her hair. She returned to the living room just as their father entered the house. He kissed her affectionately.

"You look tired," she said gently. "How was your meeting?"

"Intense," he sighed dejectedly. "Everyone knows that Kosovo is really part of Albania. The province is full of Albanians. Why won't they let the people decide what country they belong to?" His voice rose excitedly and he began to pace back and forth.

Drana wiped his troubled face gently with a large white handkerchief. "We must pray about it. But first come and have some cool moscht."

"Father! Father!" Excited voices rang from various parts of the house as the three children rushed to greet Nikola. Each competed for his attention with stories of the day. Nikola covered his ears and said laughingly, "Whoa, one at a time. I have two ears, but I can only hear one of you at a time."

A short time later, the entire family was kneeling in front of a statue of the Blessed Mother in the family living room as Drana led them in the daily Rosary. "And Blessed Mother, please ask your Son to bless Kosovo and let God's will be done there and in Skopje, in Albania, and everywhere on earth."

"Amen," the others said earnestly.

The next evening the children sat at the top of the stairs eavesdropping as Nikola's friends sat around the kitchen table discussing the tense political situation. Agnes loved and admired her father. He was attractive with dark hair and eyes, a muscular build and energetic walk. She also liked his friends, but their excitement and intensity sometimes frightened her. They tried to outshout each other in an effort to sway the group, and their passion was evident. Their voices became louder and louder and more urgent and the children's eyes grew wider, and their hearts more apprehensive. The men were excited. "We can't give up until we've won," Nikola exploded. "Kosovo must be free."

Some hours later, Drana told her husband, "I wish you didn't have to go to Belgrade."

"Drana, you know how important this dinner meeting is. We are winning important allies to our cause."

She did not reply, but nodded her head, shut her eyes and held him close.

Drana was a diligent worker who got up early each day to clean her house and care for her children. But each afternoon, before her beloved Nikola arrived from work, she would take time to freshen up a bit and change clothes. Then she would greet him at the door with a warm, tender smile.

Mother Teresa would say later, "They had a tremendous, delicate love for one another."

When Nikola returned from his dinner meeting the next evening, he opened the door abruptly and walked woodenly into the living room. Drana rose to welcome him but stopped in puzzlement as he wove his way across the room in a desperate attempt to reach her.

"Nikola," she cried as he began coughing up blood. The children came running and watched in silence as their mother knelt over Nikola's crumpled body on the floor.

"Agnes," Drana said, "run to Sacred Heart for a priest!"

The child was hit with the reality of the situation. Her beloved father was near death. She slipped out of her nightgown into her school uniform, neatly laid out for her to wear to school in the morning. Agnes had never before left the house alone after dark. The church was on the same street, only a block and a half away, but her heart beat rapidly as she ran, pushing herself to run faster, faster. Her precious father was dying. It was up to her to see that he received the Last Sacraments of his beloved church.

Out of breath, she pounded on the door of the rectory with all her strength. "Please, dear God, please help us!" she prayed. She breathed a sigh of relief as the door opened. But her heart sank as the housekeeper began to speak. "I'm sorry, child. Father is out of town. He should be home late tonight."

Her heart still pounding, Agnes ran to the Skopje Railway Station thinking Father might be on his way home. "You've got to help me, God," she prayed. The station was nearly deserted, but seated on a bench, waiting for the next train, was a tall, thin priest she had never seen before. "Father," she said, running towards him, "please come with me. My father is dying. You've got to help." Immediately the priest stood up and the two of them began to run. He was carrying a suitcase and ran awkwardly.

Drana was relieved to see them. Nikola was alive, but barely. Agnes' mission was successful and Drana was grateful. The priest gave Nikola the Last Rites, but the dying man was so weak that he could barely raise his head. He smiled briefly as his family spoke a few soft words to the priest. The unknown priest blessed the family and quietly excused himself to slip off to his train as Drana made arrangements to transport Nikola to the nearby hospital.

The hospital doctors worked feverishly over the now still form of Nikola Bojaxhiu. In the waiting room, the family suffered the hours that ticked excruciatingly and ominously by. The children had never seen their father sick. Agnes whimpered and tears rolled down her cheeks while the three children huddled together as if to shut out the unwanted reality. In a separate chair, Drana, her hands folded in her lap, prayed silently for the best and steeled herself for the worst. Pulling together the last of her reserves, she brought out her Rosary and quietly led her children into the familiar routine of their daily prayers.

It was very late when one of the weary doctors entered the small room. His eyes were downcast and his manner deliberate as he mopped his sweat-soaked brow. "I am so sorry, Mrs. Bojaxhiu. We did all we could." The girls gasped.

Lazar, his fists clenched, leapt to his feet, shouting, "Murdered! My father was murdered!" His eyes were red and swollen and he choked back tears. "I know he was murdered by the police because he was trying to free Kosovo! They killed him!"

Aga buried her face in Drana's lap while Agnes cried uncontrollably. Drana, a far-off expression on her face, was numbed by it all. After a few minutes, a new strength seemed to envelop Drana as she wiped away her own tears and called her children around her. "It's so hard to lose the people we love," she told them. "But feeling sorry they died is really being selfish. Dying is going home to Our Father. We know your Papa is up in heaven with Our Lady and Jesus. He is enjoying God's love. Let us try to be happy for him." She now had the children's undivided attention and her voice grew stronger. "We must be strong like Nikola. We have to keep our family together. We have to remember God is our Father and He is taking care of us. We have to trust Him." The children bravely nodded in acquiescence. And Drana took them home and tucked them into bed, something she had not done since they were very small.

Before Nikola died, the family had been fairly well-off financially. They lived in one of the two spacious houses they owned, and they had a lovely garden with flowers and fruit trees. They had always had a comfortable life, but when Nikola died, the situation changed almost overnight.

A few months following the death, Mr. Morten, Nikola's business partner, came to the Bojaxhiu living room to talk with Drana. "The business is off a frightening percentage, Mrs. Bojaxhiu. I've had to let most of our employees go," he said while hoisting a tea cup and trying unsuccessfully to cross his fat legs. He was a rotund individual with small, hard eyes. Drana found herself ashamed of thinking that his girth suggested he had never been forced to miss a meal.

"But I thought the business was doing well," Drana stammered. "Nikola always said . . ."

"Ah, Nikola!" The man added a deep sigh, attempting to mask his disdain. "I'm afraid your husband was a dreamer . . . never paid attention to the business. No, he had to be gallivanting all over the countryside talking politics. If he had stayed out of political talk, he would probably still be alive today . . . I worked my fingers to the bone trying to save our accounts with little or no help."

Drana scrutinized his near-obese face with its shining forehead topped with wisps of thin hair, and braced herself for what she felt was coming next. "What exactly are you saying, Mr. Morten?"

He cleared his throat and placed his tea cup in its saucer. "Madam," he began haltingly. "I've had to sell off all our holdings . . . just to pay our debts. It is going to cost me even my own personal savings . . ."

"Are you saying there is no money?" Drana asked incredulously.

"I'm afraid it's true, Mrs. Bojaxhiu. There is no pretty way of saying it . . . the business has gone broke."

"But my family . . . we are depending on the business."

"You have my deepest sympathy, Madam. But there is nothing I can do. My lawyer will contact you in a few days. Good afternoon."

Mr. Morten retrieved his wide-brimmed hat and placed it on his balding pate as he headed out the front door of the house.

Drana, completely stunned, stared at the couch where his portly figure had left an indentation in the cushions. She was desperately trying not to believe what she had just heard. She was on her knees praying when the children arrived home. She gathered them together around the dining room table, and blurted out the news.

"But how will we live without Father's business?" Lazar asked.

"Our Heavenly Father is always with us," Drana reminded them. "We will put our hands in His and walk all the way with Him."

"There is something rotten in all this, Mother," said Lazar. "Father's business was doing okay. They're stealing it from us . . ."

"I know, child," she said. "But we are not experienced in the ways of business and it will be impossible for us to prove it. It can only be that God does not wish us to have the business. He must have other plans for us. We will survive somehow through His grace."

Months later, passing the building that had housed their father's business, Aga, Lazar and Agnes spotted the large sign nailed to the front door that read: CLOSED. No words were exchanged but their disheartened expressions spoke volumes. It was not long after that afternoon that Drana was forced to sell the house next door and thereby forfeit the rent money which had been their income since Nikola's death. They sold some of the furniture, a couple of valuable clocks, and some pieces of Drana's jewelry that had been gifts from her parents and from Nikola.

"Why did Papa have to die?" Lazar cried out in frustration, watching their possessions being loaded on a cart.

"Hush, son," a calm and resolute Drana demanded. "They are only things. The important thing is that we have each other."

"Mother," Lazar said bravely, "I will leave school and find work."

The other two children echoed his offer, causing Drana to smile cryptically. "Listen, all of you," she spoke crisply with no uncertainty. "Our Heavenly Father has blessed you children with excellent minds and He expects you to make the best of His gifts. To do otherwise would be an insult to Him, a sign you don't trust Him to take care of your earthly needs."

"But, Mother," Lazar started.

"There will be no more talk of quitting school. Your father always said, 'You are never to forget that you are members of the Bojaxhiu family and you must be worthy of the name!'"

Late that night, long after the children were fast asleep, Drana, restless and unable to close her eyes, racked her tired brain, trying desperately to think of some way to keep her family together in comfort so that the children could continue growing up with only the normal burdens of childhood. Determined to be strong for the sake of her children, she said, "Blessed Mother, hclp mc to create a Nazareth where I can raise my little ones that you love even more than I. Please show me what the Lord wants me to do."

The answer was not readily forthcoming, but in the ensuing days Aga made an off-hand remark about how "tattered" their clothing was becoming.

"I'm sorry, children," Drana sighed, "I've been so preoccupied lately I've forgotten my sewing." The words were scarcely out of her mouth when her eyes lit up. "Sewing!" she exclaimed aloud. "Of course. Why didn't I think of it before? I can sew and I know cloth as well as anyone. I'll make clothes and I'll embroider and sell rugs. They're always popular!"

Weeks later, she put up a large sign in front of the Bojaxhiu home: CLOTH FOR SALE. A steady stream of ladies brought in embroidered and sewn items for her to sell.

One afternoon between sales, Drana entertained the elderly manager of one of Skopje's most prestigious garment factories. The front room was a veritable storefront with cloth samples, and hand-embroidered items on small tables everywhere. The old man admired the work he saw. "If you can spare the time to come down to the factory, Mrs. Bojaxhiu, I'd like you to look over our entire line," he said while sipping tea. "Of course, we will compensate you for any advice you give us that we can use."

"Of course," Drana replied unemotionally, "I'd be more than happy to."

Peering around the doorway, Agnes felt proud of the new-found prominence of her determined and industrious mother.

The years slipped by and the Bojaxhiu family prospered with each one. The children, a bit taller, and definitely more matured by their experiences, still missed their father, but the hurt was lessened by time. One day, Agnes came home to find Drana assisting an old woman through the front door.

"My own family doesn't want me," the old woman was whimpering in a weak voice. "How could they do this to me?"

"I'm glad you're home, Agnes." Drana said, easing the old woman onto the sofa. "I need you to help me prepare your room for our sick neighbor."

Agnes looked at the old woman with an anxious expression. Her mother motioned for Agnes to follow her as she went upstairs to Agnes' room.

"She has a tumor," Drana said as she went about her task, "and she is very ill. If we don't take care of her, she will die."

Agnes' face turned white. "How is it possible for a family not to want their own grandmother because she is ill?"

Noting Agnes' distress, Drana stopped turning down the blanket and led the child to a chair, where she took her daughter's hands in her own. Drana whispered softly and with compassion, "It is an awful thing for a family to do, turning their back on them when they are very sick or in trouble, but human beings are weak and do fall into such sins from time to time. Our Lord tells us we are not to judge or condemn anyone. If we want Our Lord's compassion we must show compassion to our brothers and sisters on this earth. Such actions remind us that the way you live your life is your religion. Jesus didn't just talk and say pretty words. He lived what He talked about. He put His words into action. Love is doing. How can we say we love Jesus, whom we have never seen, and yet not love this creature of God's, whom we see every day? Do you understand, child?"

"Of course, Mother," Agnes said.

"Good. You can move in with your sister for a while."

Drana went back to the task at hand, then almost as an afterthought turned to her daughter. "Agnes, I know I don't tell you children nearly enough how much I appreciate you. The days are so busy. There sometimes just isn't time for hugging and kissing the way your father used to."

"That's all right, Mother," Agnes answered unsteadily, not really understanding at all.

"Have you heard?" Lazar asked excitedly some hours later as he encountered Agnes sitting on Aga's bed in deep thought.

"No. What?" she asked him absent-mindedly.

"I'm going away to military school. Isn't that great?"

For a few minutes, his voice didn't seem to sink in; then a shocked Agnes slid off the bed and scrutinized Lazar as though seeing him for the first time.

"Military school?" she asked in a hollow voice.

"Yes," he said proudly, "Mother has given me her permission and I have a scholarship."

He watched for a sign of approval from his sister with a big grin on his handsome face and was greatly puzzled when he received none.

"What's the matter?" he asked, finally noting her deep sorrow.

"You're going away?" she asked. "You're leaving home?"

"Yes, Agnes. You know we've always talked about it."

"Yes," she said with a hurt expression. "But I didn't think it would be so soon."

Aga entered the room in time to hear the gist of the discussion.

"Congratulations, Lazar," she said. "Father would be so proud."

Aga hugged her brother, and Lazar looked to Agnes, who, after long moments, followed suit.

"Don't worry," he told her, "I'll be home before you know it, holidays and all."

"Sure," Agnes said wistfully.

The days before Lazar's departure seemed to whisk by much too swiftly for the girls, and one morning the little family found itself standing on a platform at the train station bidding the young man good-bye. He embraced his mother and two sisters and told them he'd miss them.

"Will you write?" Agnes asked. Tears welled up in her bright eyes.

"Of course I will," Lazar answered, trying to hold back his own tears.

Soon the old train was puffing steam as it pulled out of the station.

"First Papa. Now Lazar," Agnes mused as they waved good-bye.

"Lazar's coming back," Aga said, trying to sound cheerful.

"The time will pass faster than you can imagine," Drana promised.

The days turned into months, and the old woman that Drana had taken in miraculously prospered after countless hot meals, warm baths, fervent prayers and kind words. Her health and her strength finally returned. One glorious morning she found herself well enough to seek her own lodgings.

"How can I ever thank you, Drana?" she asked. "You saved my life." She packed her few meager belongings.

"To see you well and healthy is thanks enough," Drana replied with a smile.

Agnes, reading a book nearby, watched as the old woman left the house. "Will she be all right now, Mother?" Agnes asked.

"That's in God's hands, Agnes. He's the only One who knows."

With Nikola's death and Lazar away at school, Drana, Aga and Agnes put most of their energy into their church activities. They attended daily Mass whenever possible. Their home became a sort of religious center with people gathering together to pray, plan church festivals, practice religious plays and help those in need. Both Agnes and Aga joined the Catholic Sodality Movement dedicated to the Blessed Virgin Mary. They eagerly attended all the meetings and especially enjoyed listening to the enthusiastic letters from missionaries telling about their work, spreading the Gospel and sharing Jesus' love throughout the world.

At a church meeting, young Agnes heard one of the missionaries, a Jesuit priest who had been working in India, speak. He spoke with great passion. His words changed her life.

"Most Indians go to bed hungry every night of their lives. Many of them do not know anything about Jesus' love. They feel that no one cares about them."

The thought of masses of people starving to death was not only repugnant to Agnes, but something that had never even occurred to her as a possibility.

On the walk home, Aga asked, "Agnes, how is it possible that people could live their whole lives and die on the street, always hungry, and hot or cold, thirsty and sick?"

"That's like trying to figure out why Our Blessed Lord had to suffer and die on the cross. It's a mystery," Agnes said. She sighed deeply and her mind returned to its trance.

The priest had said, "Each person has to follow his own road."

Agnes wondered what road God had chosen for her.

The First Calling

Everyone loved Agnes. She had a rich sense of humor and kept all around her laughing. She was kind, considerate and compassionate, the friend who was always there when needed. Agnes had always given her father reason to be proud. A top student in all her classes, she was generous, kind and helpful at home. Like her older sister, she was a soloist in the church choir with a voice many compared to a nightingale. Her mother too was pleased with her baby. She loved Agnes' tender heart, her obedience, her passionate love of the Lord, and her ability to concentrate.

The parents had agreed that Agnes would make a good wife for some man and a good mother for his children. Drana was eagerly looking forward to grandchildren. When Agnes and her sister Aga walked through the streets of Skopje, the young men in the town were beginning to notice their graceful carriage, joyful nature and handsomely-made clothes.

Lorenz Antoni, their second cousin, was especially impressed by Agnes' talent as a poet and journalist and by her lovely voice in the church choir. He greatly admired her intellectual quickness, strong will, enthusiasm, and creativity. He saw something unique in her and knew that she would never be ordinary. Agnes and Lorenz would sometimes share paragraphs from their diaries and Agnes loved to hear how Lorenz tried to fathom the deep, passionate emotions that music aroused in him. She often wondered how other people saw life, how they thought, and what they wondered about. Lorenz provoked her thinking and encouraged her to search more deeply for answers. Lorenz was the only one Agnes was not afraid to share her diary with. He never made fun of anything she said and he seemed to understand what she wrote. She loved her cousin's sensitivity, his love of beauty, his devotion to the Lord and the way he encouraged her in everything she did.

Lorenz, who later became a well-known musician and composer, had his own mandolin orchestra and taught Agnes to play the mandolin. He wrote music, played several instruments, inspired her to use her writing talent and persuaded her to publish two articles in the local newspaper. At one time, Lorenz was giving mandolin lessons to three girls in the neighborhood and would not think of asking them for payment. Agnes told him, "Take a dinar from each of them for each lesson and give it to me for the missions in India."

Agnes was sometimes unhappy walking down the winding streets of Skopje, sitting quietly in the family living room, kneeling in the flower garden or climbing the hills beyond the town. "What am I doing for Jesus? Do I even know what He wants me to do? Am I truly ready to follow Him when I should hear His voice calling?" Dreams and restless thoughts kept disturbing her peace. She was beginning to feel that the love of her family was not enough. Something was missing in her life. She was not even sure what it was, but she could feel the empty place in her soul. And she was beginning to know that only God could fill it, although she had no idea how He would do it or when or where. She thought of great saints like Joan of Arc and St. Paul, whose life stories she had read, those who gave their lives for their faith, who were slaughtered and tortured in all sorts of terrible ways. Part of her longed to die for God. Another part was repulsed by the idea. But she always ended with, "Lord, I am Yours. Do whatever You want with me." Then she would feel at peace for awhile. She would feel confident that God would soon speak to her, tell her exactly what He wanted. When she failed to hear His voice, she felt an emptiness deep inside her and she wondered once more.

When God did speak to her, it was through a Jesuit priest, Father Jambrenkovic, a man strongly identified with the Albanian cause just as her father had been. This priest had great zeal for the missions and shared his enthusiasm with the young people of the parish. It was he who had introduced the missionary priest from India to his parish when Agnes was twelve.

Now, six years later, Father Jambrenkovic once again spoke of the conditions in India and how parishioners could help. As he spoke, everything began to make sense to Agnes. There was no hesitation. God was calling her to be a missionary. She felt her heart fill with joy. "Yes, Lord," she whispered. "Of course, I'll follow You wherever You say."

She went to her cousin Lorenz and asked, "How can you know if God is calling you? And if He is calling you, how do you know for sure what He is calling you to?"

Lorenz looked very serious. "I remember Father Jambrenkovic saying that when you think God is calling you, you should feel great joy. That great joy is the sign of a vocation."

"Oh, I feel great joy," she told him. "I have never felt such joy. It is as if a great burden were lifted. I feel joy." She paused a minute and tears ran down her cheeks. "Oh, I do feel great joy. But it is going to be so hard going away, leaving Skopje. I may never see my mother again, or Aga, or Lazar, or you . . ."

"I always thought we'd grow old together," said Lorenz. "Even after we both got married, we would stay best friends. We are cousins and we have shared our diaries and our poetry and our secret dreams . . ."

"I will miss you," Agnes said.

"I will miss you too," he said. "But, Agnes, will your mother let you go?"

"You know my mother," Agnes said. "She would never say no to Jesus."

The next day, Agnes told Father Jambrenkovic, "I feel God calling me to be a missionary. I believe He wants me to serve Him in India."

The priest studied the young girl for a moment, then told her, "There are some Irish nuns who work mainly in India. I will recommend you to their order."

"Oh, thank you, Father!"

When Agnes returned home, she went into the kitchen where her mother was bent over the sink, cutting vegetables. She stood behind her in silence until Drana sensed her presence. "Is that you, Agnes?" her mother asked. "Then tell me what you are up to."

"Mother, I am convinced that God is calling me to give my life to Him, to serve Him in foreign lands. If I am not mistaken, He wants me to be a missionary in India. You have always told me to trust Him, so I know that you will give me your blessing."

Agnes looked at her mother's face. It had turned pale and had an expression she had never seen before. Slowly, Drana put down the potato she was paring, straightened the mess from the peelings, covered the pot with a clean dish towel and left the room without saying a word. Agnes stood silent, watching her mother climb the stairs to her bedroom. She heard her footsteps in the hallway—precise, slow and constant. She heard her mother's bedroom door open and close. Agnes waited.

She prayed, "God, You have called me to follow You as a missionary. Surely You can reassure my mother. You can help her to accept this great change as You are helping me. Please, dear God, don't let my actions cause pain to my dear mother. Let her hear Your Voice. Please."

Agnes slipped into the kitchen chair where her mother often sat. She stared out at the evening sky, at the mountains in the distance, the hills of home. Did they have hills in India? Of course, some of the highest mountains in the world. The Himalayas. She wondered what part of India she would be sent to. Then she remembered how far from Skopje she would be going, and how she might never again see her village, nor her wonderful, loving relatives and friends. Never again to see anyone she had known her entire life. Could she bear it? No wonder her beloved mother had been so affected by the news.

When she looked at the sky again, it was black. There were stars shining everywhere. Still no sounds coming from her mother's room. Was she crying? Agnes had never seen her mother crying, not even when her father died. She had cried then, Agnes knew, because each time Drana came out of the bedroom, her eyes were red. Several times Agnes had found her mother with tears on her cheeks, but she had not made a sound in front of the children. Probably she was praying, perhaps saying a Rosary, asking the Holy Spirit to let her know His will for Agnes' life. Agnes sat staring out the window as the hours passed. She began saying her own Rosary. Even at age eighteen, the Rosary was very central to her life. She loved meditating on the scenes from Jesus' life as she recited the Ave Marias.

Agnes was still saying her Rosary when Aga touched her shoulder. She jumped. "What's the matter, Agnes?" her sister asked. "You're not your normal peaceful self. Something awful is on your mind. And where is mother? Hasn't she even started to get dinner ready? It's almost seven. I thought I'd be in trouble for being late."

"Mother's in her room."

"Is she sick? Have you checked on her? It must be serious. I can't ever remember coming home and dinner wasn't ready or almost ready."

Aga started up the stairs towards her mother's bedroom.

"Wait a minute, Aga!" Agnes called. "I think Mother wants to be alone. Come, sit down and we'll talk."

A puzzled Aga looked at her sister.

"Aga, you know I've always thought God might be calling me to be a missionary. I have been praying about it and I have spoken with Father Jambrenkovic. He agrees with me and he feels I do have a vocation. He told me to pray some more and to discuss it with Mother."

"And that's what is going on with Mother?" Aga said. "What did you tell her?"

"What I told you."

"And what did she say?"

"Nothing. She went directly to her room. That was hours ago."

The two sisters decided it was past time for preparing the dinner. They finished cutting the vegetables and put them on to boil. When the food was ready, it was almost bedtime and their mother had not left her room, nor had she spoken a word to either of them. Drana stayed in her room for twenty-four hours without speaking. It was late afternoon when she slowly opened her bedroom door and started down the stairs. Agnes watched her mother's slow, deliberate steps and tried to decipher the meaning of the complete lack of expression. Her mouth felt dry, her hands cold. "Dear Lord, please let my mother understand. Let her give her blessing. She taught me to love You. She taught me always to listen to You. Please help!"

"My little Gonxha," her mother said when she saw her standing at the bottom of the stairs. "I wish I could keep you with me always," she said, caressing Agnes' face. "But I see that in your heart you have already left us."

She took Agnes' hand and led her to the sofa. "Come, let us make plans. There is much to do before you leave for your journey."

"Thank you, Mother, for being so understanding," Agnes said, a huge burden lifted from her chest.

"Just keep your hand in Jesus' hand," her mother said. "Follow Him all the way."

Drana made a list of all the duties Agnes should do before leaving home. The first was to write a letter to her brother.

That year, Albania had became a monarchy under King Zog I, and Lazar, having graduated from the military academy in Tirana, had been promoted to lieutenant. In her letter, she told him of her plans to become a nun.

His reply shocked her: "How could a girl like you become a nun? Do you realize you are burying yourself?" Agnes was sorely disappointed that her brother did not share her great joy. She wrote back, "You think you are so important as an official serving the King of two million subjects. Well, I shall be an official too, serving the King of the whole world!"

When Agnes told her cousin Lorenz she was going away to be a nun, he asked, "When are you leaving?"

"Next week," she told him.

"You work fast," he said, smiling at her.

"It is God's work," she told him. "He's my King now. He has always been my King, of course. Now it is official."

"We will miss you. Our lives will be much less interesting without your cheerful smile, your enthusiasm and sense of humor. I'm so glad we are cousins . . . there will be a link between us even when we are apart."

"God's love links all of us together," she told him.

The young people of the church Sodality and Choir had a concert and dedicated the last section to Agnes as their farewell.

Before she left, Agnes went through her closet, preparing all of her clothes to give to the poor. It was like stepping into a time machine and going back into her past. Each dress brought its own memories and its own emotions.

"What kind of memories will I be making in the future?" she wondered. How strange it was to think that she would not be wearing pretty dresses ever again. Soon her entire wardrobe would consist of the Loreto nun's habit, a long black gown with long sleeves and a large white collar. Her hair would be cut off and she would always wear a veil over her head. Before it had all seemed so abstract. Now it was becoming real and part of her reached out eagerly for it, but the other part wondered just where her life was headed. When she left the boxes at the church, she felt as though she were leaving a part of herself behind. "Let it be the frivolous part of me that I leave," she thought.

She took a long last look at the church and headed home. "Please, God, let me keep my love of laughter, my love of learning and my love of life. Even if I'm to dress somberly at all times, let me know the joy of my vocation."

On September 25th, Drana and Aga had a going-away party for Agnes. Many of her friends brought gifts. Lorenz gave her a gold fountain pen. "Maybe you won't be a famous writer," he laughed, "but you can continue your diary. And once in awhile I would like a letter."

That night Agnes found it difficult to sleep. The excitement of finally realizing her dream, coupled with the sadness of leaving everything familiar, was nearly overwhelming, but Agnes persisted in her determination not to let her fears overcome her. With this in mind she drifted off into the light from a bright September moon, which transfixed her as though some distant spotlight were expecting a performance. The voices of Aga, Drana and Lazar drifted about the room.

Drana: "You'll do fine, child. Just keep your faith in the Almighty and remember that you have family here who loves you."

Aga: "I'm going to miss you. Come back soon. I will be praying for you."

Lazar: "You're burying yourself . . . burying yourself . . . burying."

It seemed to Agnes that she had hardly shut her eyes when Drana knocked on the door.

"I'm not burying myself . . . I'm not burying myself . . . " Agnes mumbled, still half asleep.

"What's that you are saying?" Drana asked as she entered the small bedroom.

Agnes slowly focused her eyes on her mother. "Nothing, Mother, I must have been dreaming."

"Well, come on. Get up. Your breakfast is ready. You don't want to be late for the train."

A short time later, Agnes, Drana and Aga were once again at the train station, this time preparing for Agnes' good-bye. Agnes was surprised to see that a large crowd had gathered to wish her well. Most of her classmates were there along with many parishioners of Sacred Heart church. Agnes knew that everyone was looking at her and wondering what her future held. Lorenz approached her. Drana opened her purse and pulled out some money which she handed to him. "Please get three tickets to Zagreb for us, nephew." (Drana and Aga were going with her for the first part of the journey.) Happy to have something to do, Lorenz hurried to the ticket counter.

When he returned, he and Agnes stood close to each other. They each had so much to say, so many memories to recount, so much encouragement they had shared. Finally, they both said good-bye at the same time and smiled tearfully. Agnes pressed Lorenz' hand tightly. Tears streaked her face as she followed her mother and sister inside the train. She waved her handkerchief out the window while the train pulled out of the station, leaving her friends and childhood behind.

In Belgrade, Agnes and her family waited for the train to Zagreb. Agnes had so many things she wanted to say to them, but one thought chased the next away before the words were formed. And so all three sat in silence.

They had been traveling for eight hours on the train to Belgrade and another eight hours on the train to Zagreb. They slept restlessly and felt exhausted, both physically and mentally. When they pulled into the train station at Zagreb, however, it was much too soon for any of them.

"Are you sure you have enough money?" Drana asked.

"Yes, Mother," Agnes answered with a new-found calmness.

"You better write every day," Aga said, fighting back the tears.

"I will if I can. I promise," Agnes said.

Drana and Aga each held Agnes in their arms and hugged her so tightly she thought she would fall over from lack of air. Then they quickly left the train. Agnes looked out the window at the two women she loved most in the world. They seemed small and forlorn waving their good-byes.

Agnes met Betike Kanjc, the young woman the nuns had arranged for her to travel with. The two women were to go to the Loreto House in Paris, where Mother Eugene MacAvin, the Sister in charge, would interview them. If she recommended them to the Mother General, they would go to the Mother House in Ireland for training and then on to India. Agnes and Betike stared out of the window as the train rolled across Austria finally bringing them to Paris, their first step to becoming missionaries in India.

In Paris, the two young women saw businessmen at their trade, shopkeepers selling their wares, people sightseeing and enjoying the city, priests crossing the streets, women in tight-fitting clothes and heavy makeup standing on street corners, mourners on their way to a funeral, lovers walking hand-in-hand stopping to kiss in the shade of a tree. They saw mothers trying to control their children and schoolchildren walking home from school in their uniforms.

"Just where do I fit in?" Agnes wondered. "God, are You calling me to live behind walls and dedicate all my thoughts to You? If that is Your wish, let me know. Let me be certain and I will be faithful in thought, word and deed."

Agnes had one single goal, to lose herself and find her Lord, to become empty of desires, hopes, thoughts, dreams and feelings that were not directly from God. She wanted her mind and heart and soul to know the peace that passes all understanding and to know the restlessness and thirst for God that leads to perfect love.

When they knocked on the door of the large old building in Paris where the Loreto Sisters lived, Agnes and Betike were both breathless and scared. Agnes prayed that she would not destroy God's plan for her by saying the wrong words, using the wrong tone or having the wrong expression. "God, I have longed to adore You completely as a nun. If this is Your will, please help me."

They were invited inside and ushered into a large, simply furnished room where they were told to sit down on a plain but comfortable sofa. Agnes was already getting homesick for her family and wondered if she was mistaken, if maybe God was calling her to do something in Skopje, closer to home.

"How weak I am," she reprimanded herself, "to doubt my calling at the first obstacle. I offer the homesickness to You, my God. Please show me what You want me to do."

Mother Eugene came into the room with an interpreter from the Yugoslavian Embassy. She asked Agnes, "Do you feel certain God is calling you to be a nun?"

"Yes, Mother," Agnes said. "I do feel certain."

"And how do you know He is calling you?"

"Because of the great joy I feel knowing He wants me to serve Him as a missionary. Ever since I became sure of the call I have felt this great joy, this peace . . ."

But as she said the words, she realized that at that moment all of her joy and all of her peace seemed to escape her and she felt only the sorrow at leaving her beloved family. She was unable to prevent a deep sob. Mother Eugene put her arms around her.

"My dear, I know it is difficult leaving your home, your family. I remember how I felt when I left mine."

"But I do want to leave," Agnes said, trying to smile through her tears. "I know God wants me to be a missionary in India and I never say no to Him."

Mother Eugene recommended the girls and sent them to the Loreto Abbey at

Rathfarnham, Dublin, the Mother House for training. Dublin, Ireland, was three times the size of Skopje, and Agnes marveled at the vastness. Yet, at the same time, traveling by horse and cart, she was struck by the similarities, the many farms, the herds of sheep, the rolling hills. Betike must have had the same thought for she said, "It looks so much like home."

The weather was brisk as the countryside readied itself for the onslaught of winter and Agnes clutched her coat collar to her throat, warding off the chill. Her eyes narrowed themselves involuntarily against the swirling dust from the bumpy dirt roads. At last they arrived at the convent, and the elderly driver snapped Agnes out of her reverie: "Here we are, my little lasses, all safe and sound." He swung down from the cart and reached for their valises in the rear baggage section. It was then that Agnes noticed the large building that housed the convent and the kindly-faced nun standing at the front gate.

"Agnes Gonxha Bojaxhiu and Betike Kanjc?" the nun asked.

Agnes and Betike were examining the immense structure with wide eyes. They turned to face the little nun. "Yes, Sister," Agnes said.

"You must be tired after such a long journey. Come, there is food and water inside." She assisted the two girls with their valises and together they entered the building. The girls did not understand much of the woman's conversation since it was in English but her kindly attitude was most welcome. Agnes and Betike were directed to their modest quarters and a short time later were in the dining room eating supper. Absolutely famished, they truly enjoyed the food, cooked cabbage with potatoes and homemade bread.

After they finished eating, a young nun took them through several hallways until they reached a pleasant but business-like office, a spacious room with book-shelves lining two entire walls. Behind a modest desk, an elderly white-haired Sister sat looking at them over her glasses and smiling. She began to give what Agnes took to be a warm welcoming speech but neither girl knew enough English to understand.

In the ensuing days, Agnes and Betike immersed themselves in English classes. A born hard worker and a lover of details, Agnes learned rapidly. Her friend was not far behind and at times even surpassed Agnes in learning vocabulary and the use of verbs in a sentence. But never for a moment did Agnes forget Skopje and all the loved ones she had left behind.

"What's the matter? Homesick?" Betike asked with a smile as she entered Agnes' tiny cell one evening.

"Yes, a little," Agnes admitted, leaning her face on her hand over a just-completed letter, "but I'm determined to do God's will. He called me here for a reason. I just know it."

"I'm sure He did, Agnes. You'll know what it is soon."

"I went to the town square yesterday. It is almost like being back home except that the people speak a different language."

"Speaking of that, how's your English coming along?"

In response, Agnes recited an English limerick almost flawlessly. Her friend giggled with delight. Each day the girls worked at their language studies and did their share of cleaning, washing dishes and various duties as they were assigned.

One night, Agnes wrote to Drana that she was finally realizing her dream of being a missionary. She and Betike were being sent to India. Betike sat nearby, sad-faced with ambivalent emotions. She too had long dreamed of being a missionary, and yet she dreaded the idea of being even further from her home.

After six weeks in Ireland, on November 28, 1928, Agnes and Betike boarded the *Marcha* for India. Ireland would always tug at their hearts. Although neither girl had been close to any of the novitiates or the nuns since none of them spoke Serbo-Croatian or Albanian, there was a bond of love that united them and both girls had felt very much at home in the convent.

The ship sailed at 4:00 in the afternoon. The sea was calm and the air smelled fresh. The hills of Ireland rose up in the background. Agnes and Betike shared a cabin that was just a bit smaller than the cells they'd each had in the convent.

They soon met three young Franciscan Sisters who were also going to India. "Let's plan our lives the way it is in the convent," one of the Franciscan Sisters suggested. We'll get up at 5:00 a.m., meet for prayer at 5:50 and go to breakfast together at 7:00." They had all their meals together and they planned prayer and meditation times as well as a recreation period each day.

The trip was to last seven weeks. The ship would go through the Suez Canal, the Red Sea, the Indian Ocean, and finally the Bay of Bengal. On the sea, the nights were beautiful with the moon shining on the sparkling waves. But the days were long and tiresome, and when storms rocked the ship, tossing it from side to side, Agnes and her friends fought off seasickness.

They were disappointed to learn that there was not a single Catholic priest on board. It was a long journey and they especially disliked the idea of not being able to receive Holy Communion on Christmas. Determined to have a joyful Christmas even though they would be unable to attend Mass, the Sisters improvised a manger scene from cardboard. Agnes spent hours praying to the Baby Jesus, asking Him to prepare her for her life's work. Every day they sang Christmas carols. On Christmas Eve they recited the Rosary together before the crib at midnight and ended their evening singing "Adeste Fideles." It was a beautiful star-spangled night and the ocean glowed in the moonlight.

It was her first Christmas away from home and Agnes felt very homesick, but Betike and the three Franciscan nuns were her sisters in Christ and their fellowship was consoling. It cheered her to realize that her dream of being Jesus' missionary was coming true. They rejoiced when the ship stopped at Port Said since they could attend Mass and receive Holy Communion for the first time since they had left Ireland.

The ship reached Columbo, Ceylon (now Sri Lanka) on December 27, 1928. Mr. Scalon, the brother of one of the Loreto Sisters, was waiting for them at the dock. He took them to the college of St. Joseph where they found a small chapel and spent some time in prayer. Then he invited them to his home. They were amazed at the scenes they witnessed on the streets. It was easy for them to recognize Europeans in their elegant clothes while most of the natives were half-naked and bare-footed. Agnes felt sorry for the poor men who pulled their rickshaws through the crowded streets as she was used to seeing horses pulling carts and wagons. Mr. Scalon decided to bring the girls to his house in a rickshaw and the five of them reluctantly got in. They all prayed that the load would not be too uncomfortable for their poor driver and they breathed a joyful sigh when the short trip was over.

They spent the next day touring Columbo and at 7:30 in the evening they returned to the ship, grateful to learn that a Jesuit priest was on board, on his way to India. Now they would have daily Mass.

New Year's Eve was a festive occasion even though Agnes and her friends all felt homesick. They each remembered the wonderful times shared with family back home.

Late in the afternoon on New Year's Day, the ship arrived at Madras. Agnes got her first sad view of the poor of India from the deck of the ship. The next day, she and her friends visited the city and could not believe how poor the people were. The streets were covered with homeless families who slept on mats woven from palm leaves (they were the lucky ones), on old rags or, in many cases, on the bare ground. Agnes thought, "If the people back home could see this they would never complain about anything. They would praise God for all His blessings."

Many of the people were completely naked. Some men were bare-chested with a simple loincloth. Often the very poor wore finely-worked bracelets on their arms and legs with earrings and a nose ring. On their foreheads were special marks that had religious significance.

On January 6, 1929, the Feast of the Three Kings, the ship arrived in Calcutta. Agnes felt this was surely a sign from God that He gave her mission a special blessing. Their Loreto Sisters were waiting for them on the docks and their warm welcome helped Agnes and Betike feel at home in this faraway land. Their first stop was the convent chapel where they thanked God for a safe journey and asked His blessings on the rest of their lives.

After a week in Calcutta, Agnes and Betike were sent to Darjeeling, a beautiful city in the foothills of the awe-inspiring Himalayas.

"I thought it would be different," Agnes told Betike. "I've heard such terrible stories."

"Darjeeling is a resort city for the well-to-do," her friend said. "At least that is what one of the Sisters told me."

"Look at the snow on top of the mountains!" Agnes said. "It looks a lot like Skopje."

"That's what you said about Ireland," Betike joked. "Every place looks like Skopje to you."

"I think I'm going to like India," Agnes said.

When she was settled in her room that evening, Agnes was excited and curious about her new surroundings, but her exhausted body insisted on sleep.

The days in Darjeeling moved swiftly for Agnes, and almost before she realized, May had arrived, the month traditionally dedicated to the Blessed Mother. On May 23, 1929, Agnes and her friend, Betike, were accepted as novices, officially entering the Order of Loreto. Agnes was nervous with anticipation. The Archbishop of Calcutta attended the ceremony and gave the homily at Mass. He reminded the two girls that they were beginning a new life dedicated completely to God and he asked everyone present to renew his or her baptismal vows and dedicate their lives to God. Agnes and Betike approached the altar and knelt.

The Mother Superior smiled down at them and said, "As a sign of giving up your old life, you now take a new name. What will you now be called?"

Agnes had been anticipating this question for weeks. "I shall be Mary Teresa. Mary for Our Blessed Mother who lived her life in chastity, poverty and obedience, and Teresa for St. Thérèse of Lisieux, the Little Flower. She is the patron saint of missionaries and I am going to be a missionary."

Several months earlier, Agnes had come across a small book entitled *The Little*

White Flower: The Story of a Soul, the autobiography of St. Thérèse. She was intrigued by Thérèse's "little way of spiritual childhood," a path to God through complete trust and absolute self-surrender. St. Thérèse admitted in her book that she really wanted to bc a priest, an apostle, a martyr, a doctor of the Church. In Corinthians 13 and 14, St. Paul showed her how to reconcile those ambitions by understanding that only love has value. She realized her true vocation was simply to love. St. Thérèse insisted on her own "littleness" and on how it was possible for everyone to follow her little way. She saw the importance of accepting joyfully the small happenings of daily life, and she showed how all people are called to holiness.

Agnes had always loved the Bible. She loved to listen to the priest read the Gospel and Epistle at every Mass she attended. The words always touched her heart and brought her soul closer to God. After reading *The Story of a Soul*, the good news of the Gospels became even more alive for her. When she finished reading the book, Agnes vowed that she too would see her vocation as love, and she would always do little things with great love.

Agnes' friend, Betike, took Sister Mary Magdalene as her new name.

That evening Agnes wrote a letter to her Mother and one to her Aunt Maria, her cousin Lorenz' grandmother. She sent a photo to her aunt on which she wrote: "My health is good. This photo is a souvenir of the greatest day of my life in which I became all Christ's. All my love, from your Agnes, little Teresa of the Child Jesus."

Before she went to bed she prayed with great joy: "Dear Jesus, let me be as the Little Flower and love You with an all-consuming love. Let me bring as many little souls as possible home to You."

The Second Calling

Characteristically, Agnes—Sister Teresa—performed her tasks with single mindedness, finding herself increasingly busy. She had less time for writing her family, who she knew anxiously awaited every letter. She, in turn, was overjoyed whenever she received a letter from Yugoslavia. Each day, though, weaned her further from her mother's world.

On May 25, 1931, Agnes and Betike made their first temporary vows. They took the vow of Chastity to love Jesus with all their hearts, the vow of Poverty so that their only attachment would be to their Lord, the vow of Obedience to imitate Jesus in His relationship with His Father, whose will He always followed.

The novitiate period is a time of preparation for religious life. For the average young woman seeking to become a nun, the life is strange, strenuous and difficult. For Agnes and Betike, the transition was even more shocking for they had left their peaceful mountain homeland to find themselves suddenly in a land of human suffering that surpassed anything they had ever imagined. In addition, both were learning English, Bengali and Hindi.

Agnes was sent to help the nurses in a small Bengalese village hospital. Every morning before she started to work, Agnes would stop at the hospital pharmacy to admire a painting of Jesus surrounded by a crowd of sick people. She would say a quick prayer: "Lord, I offer all I do today for You and for souls."

The waiting room was always crowded with sick, hungry, unhappy people. As soon as Sister Teresa would enter the room, every eye would look at her with desperate hope. Mothers would hand her their sick babies. Sister Teresa would pray over them, speaking words of healing and consolation. Many people had open sores on their faces, hands, legs and feet. Some were in the last stages of tuberculosis. There were babies with boils on their backs as big as her fist. She told them, "Bring me the babies for whom the doctors can do no more. I have a wonderful medicine for them." When the mothers brought their babies, Sister Teresa would pray over them, asking God to heal them or give them a beautiful eternity with Him.

One day a man arrived carrying a child who looked very sick. Sister Teresa was convinced the little boy would soon be dead. The man was afraid the hospital would refuse to take the little boy, so he told Sister Teresa gruffly, "If you won't take him, I will throw him in the high grass and the jackals will take care of him for sure." She couldn't believe her ears. She took a closer look and saw that the child was blind as well as dying. She took him in her arms and held him close to her. The father left and she got holy water to baptize the child, then took him to the nurses.

Sister Teresa was very happy at the hospital and wrote a short article about the work which was published in the November 1931 issue of *Catholic Mission* in Zagreb, Yugoslavia.

She did not stay long at the mission hospital, however, for her superiors sent her to their college in Calcutta where she completed her studies and obtained her teaching certificate. In Calcutta, Sister Teresa got another glimpse of the terrible poverty that the missionaries had described. Here was a city with a damp, stifling climate, overcrowded streets and chaotic slums or bustees, as they are called in India. It was dirty and smelly, plagued with sickness and desperation. Millions of poor people lived and died on the streets without ever having a home.

The Loreto Convent was an oasis of beauty and tranquility in the center of one of the most crowded bustees. A concrete wall surrounded the convent and high school. Inside the wall, students dressed in clean, neat uniforms, learned their lessons, laughed and played in their safe, comfortable world. The well-cared-for school grounds were covered with deep green grass and swaying palm trees. From her bedroom window, Sister Teresa could see the poor people in the bustee outside the wall. She prayed for them constantly.

Some of the students at the school were orphans or children of broken marriages of all races and communities. But the majority of them came from rather well-to-do families.

Sister Teresa had an inner beauty and radiated joy and enthusiasm. She had often dreamed of teaching school. On her first day of teaching, she noticed that the children seemed afraid of her and all eyes were upon her, watching her every move. So she got water and a mop, rolled up her sleeves, moved everything out of the room and began to clean the floor. The children could not believe their eyes. Never had they seen a teacher do such a thing. This was India where the caste system was so strong and only lower caste did the cleaning. But Sister Teresa was enjoying herself and had a bright smile which intrigued them as much as her actions. Soon the girls were helping her mop and the boys were going for clean water. It took them two hours to have the room neat and clean. Then class began.

Sister Teresa's natural affinity for her students, her lively sense of humor and her ready smile quickly won their love. She was extremely popular with the other teachers as well.

On May 24, 1937, after nine years in India, Sister Teresa and Sister Mary Magdalene made their final vows at Darjeeling on the Feast of Mary, Help of

Christians. "Jesus, my love," Sister Teresa sighed, "I am now wed to You for my whole life. Please fill my heart with so much love for You that no woman in the whole world will ever love her husband as much as I love You."

After making her vows, Sister Teresa became Mother Teresa and returned to Calcutta. She taught at St. Mary's High School and soon became director of curriculum.

On September 1, 1939, Nazi Germany invaded Poland. On September 3rd, Britain declared war on Germany and, without consulting any Indians, brought India into the war. The Indian Congress, led by Mahatma Ghandi's non-violent resistance, demanded their freedom. Winston Churchill, Prime Minister of England, refused.

On December 7, 1941, the Japanese bombed Pearl Harbor and the United States entered the war. President Roosevelt tried to get Churchill to grant India her independence, but the Prime Minister again refused. Boats that once brought rice from paddy lands to the cities were forced into military service, cutting off an already meager food supply and causing a famine that took over four million lives.

During the years of the Second World War, Mother Teresa taught almost every subject: history, geography, English, and religion. "She taught religion in such a way," one of her students said later, "that everything came alive for us. We felt the love of Jesus and His sacrifices for us and the beauty of sacrificing for Him. She taught us in our Bengali language."

Mother Teresa was made principal of St. Mary's School. She was also put in charge of the Daughters of St. Anne, the Indian religious order attached to the Loreto Sisters. While she was principal, she became good friends with Father Henry, pastor of St. Teresa's Church in Entally, not far from St. Mary's School. Father Henry had been born in a coal mining town in Dampremy, Belgium, and had come to India in October 1938. When he saw the great need, he felt God's call and remained.

From 1941 to 1947, Mother Teresa and Father Henry worked together with the Sodality of Our Lady, a Catholic organization for girls from twelve to twenty. This was the same group that Teresa had joined back in Skopje as a child. Their goal was to serve the poorest of the poor and they believed in putting prayer into action. The girls visited hospitals and slums looking for ways to better serve God. Mother Teresa gave the girls aspirins, bandages, iodine, and whatever she thought might be of use to the people.

In the days before the partition of India into separate Hindu and Muslim nations, Calcutta suffered immensely because its population was almost equally divided between the two religions and they were now terrified of one another.

There were often riots.

England was ready to leave India, just waiting for the country to form their own government. Gandhi and the Indian Congress wanted a united India where people of all religions lived in peace. Muslim leaders wanted to create a separate Muslim state. They felt Muslims who were the minority in certain sections of India would be in danger if they did not have their own government. The newly-formed Muslim League declared August 16, 1946 "Direct Action Day," aggravating the hostility between the two groups.

During all this chaos, Ma Charu, a cook at St. Mary's School, came to Mother Teresa in a panic. "What will we do, Mother? The food hasn't arrived and we have 300 hungry mouths to feed."

"Pray," Teresa told her. "Pray hard."

Mother Teresa went into the streets alone, determined to buy the necessary provisions. This was the first time she had left the convent by herself and she discovered a city frozen by violence. Middle-class people were afraid to step outside their door. Businesses were closed down. Shops were set afire with their owners inside. Old people lay dying on the sidewalks. Men and women had been stabbed and left on the street to bleed to death. Bodies were tossed into sewers. It was a soul-striking experience even for one schooled in God's will.

A truckload of soldiers stopped her. "What are you doing in the street, lady? Don't you see how dangerous it is?"

"I had to come out. I have 300 students with nothing to eat."

"We have rice, lady. Get in the truck and we'll take you back to your school." The soldiers unloaded the bags of rice for her. Mother Teresa thanked them.

"Ma Charu, your prayers worked," she told the cook. Ma Charu hurried into the kitchen to prepare the rice for the hungry girls.

At least 5,000 people died that day and over 15,000 were wounded. And yet Mother Teresa wrote her mother, "I am sorry not to be with you, but you can be pleased, because your little Agnes is very happy . . . I teach and this is the work I like best. I am also in charge of the whole school and everyone here loves me."

Her mother answered her letter with this one: "My dearest daughter, do not forget that you went out there to help the poor. Do you remember old Filja? She is covered with sores but what bothers her the most is to realize that she is all alone in the world."

Mother Teresa was suspected of having tuberculosis and was sent to Darjeerling to recover. On September 10, 1946, as the train puffed its way up the mountainside, Teresa closed her eyes and images of the horrors of Calcutta passed through her mind. She saw abandoned children lying on the sidewalks ignored by passers-by. She watched living skeletons searching through garbage bins for food. She saw a mother, driven insane by hunger and despair, trying to strangle her own little boy.

"Whatever you do to the least of my people, you do to me," Teresa heard Jesus repeat over and over in her head.

On her lap she held *Imitation of Christ* by Thomas A. Kempis. It was one of Teresa's favorite books and as soon as she began reading, her mind became enchanted by the author's great love for Christ and she could feel her heart leaping as she saw herself following Him every step of His way, her own personal Way of the Cross.

Suddenly, she heard His voice. It was inside her. He was on the Cross. "I thirst," He said. "Teresa, I thirst for your love."

"My Lord, I love You," she said.

"Quench my thirst in the poorest of the poor. Follow me out of the convent and into the streets. Be my hands and tend my sick. Be my feet and visit my lonely, my sick, my prisoners. Be my voice and calm the distressed, comfort the afflicted, help the dying to come home to me."

Was she losing her mind? Jesus would never call her to do these things. He had called her to be a nun in a convent. He had called her to leave the world and follow Him on an inward journey. How could He be asking her to leave the convent and return to the world? Her superiors would never allow it, and she had taken a vow to obey God in her superiors at all times.

"Am I, a nun, threatened by tuberculosis, to leave the convent and the life I love, where I feel so close to You, and go out alone?" she asked.

And He repeated the call. "Teresa, do you love me?"

"Oh, yes, Lord."

"Then feed my sheep. Come follow me . . ."

"Yes, Lord," she whispered. First she said it in her head, then in her heart.

"Yes, my Lord. You know I love You and I always say yes to You. Whatever You ask for I will give You willingly and whatever You give me I will take willingly. I am all Yours."

"I love you, Teresa." Jesus' voice was clear and full of intense compassion. The eyes of her soul saw the way He looked at her with infinite love. Teresa was faced with Jesus' all-consuming, unconditional love for her. It was as if there was no one else in the world but Jesus and herself.

"Thank you, Jesus," she said. "Your love is all I need, all I will ever need." She knew the fire that Jesus had lit in her soul would burn forever. From it she would draw the strength to do His will for as long as she lived.

During her recuperation, Teresa was quiet and stayed to herself most of the time as she prayed and meditated. Her resolve grew stronger. She never doubted that God was calling her once more, that He was asking her to drop everything and follow Him wherever He called her.

She had never said no to Jesus and she was not going to begin now.

"What's wrong, Mother Teresa?" asked Sister Mary Magdalene, who was also in Darjeerling. "Are you ill? You are so quiet and you aren't smiling."

"I'm sorry, Sister Magdalene," she said. "I'm thinking, trying to determine exactly what God wants me to do. I think He wants me to leave the convent . . ."

Sister Mary Magdalene cut her off: "Leave the convent? God called you to the convent. He would never call you away."

"I believe that is what He is doing," Teresa said. She sighed. "I know where I belong but I don't know how to get there."

"Oh, Mother Teresa," Sister Mary Magdalene begged, "please don't do anything until you're absolutely sure you know what you are doing."

"Pray for me, Sister. Ask Our Lady to help me hear His voice and know His will."

"I'll pray for you, Sister. I promise."

Although Mother Teresa was eager to begin her new mission she could do nothing until she was released from her convent and had permission to go out into the streets where Jesus was calling her. The first thing she did was write a description of her original inspiration, the call and the repetition of the call during the retreat. She wrote plans for her future work, caring for the poor in their dwellings and in the street. The work would be done in a spirit of trust, surrender and joy. It would not be done behind walls in an institution and those who joined would be bound to satiate Jesus' thirst for souls by wholehearted and free service to the poor.

When she returned to Calcutta, she took the notes to her spiritual director, Father Celest Van Exem, a Jesuit priest who spoke Arabic and had many friends among the Muslims of Calcutta. Father Van Exem read her papers and said, "If you wish, you can write directly to Rome to ask the Congregation for the Propagation of the Faith to release you from the Sisters of Loreto. But I suggest instead that you take everything to the Archbishop and ask his help in the matter."

"That sounds best to me too, Father."

Archbishop Perier received Teresa like a true father, with kindness and understanding. He listened to her attentively. Then, he said, "I'm sorry. I must say no, absolutely no."

Mother Teresa returned to her convent and told her superior of the Archbishop's refusal. Despite her eagerness to begin her mission, she took up her regular duties and continued as though nothing had happened. But day and night she prayed that Jesus would show her exactly what He wanted her to do, and when and how. She put her complete faith in Him and knew that in His time His will would be done with her life.

1947 was a year of waiting for Mother Teresa. It was a traumatic year of bloodshed for India. On August 15, 1947, England granted India her independence, but Mahatma Gandhi, whose peaceful resistance had led India to freedom, did not celebrate. India broke out in riots as it was divided into two nations, Pakistan for the Muslims, and what was left of India for the Hindus. The border between India and the newly-formed East Pakistan cut through Bengal, and millions of Hindus and Muslims found themselves in enemy territory. There was a mass exodus as they attempted to get to where they were safe, and as a result, millions of Hindu refugees fleeing East Pakistan poured into the already over-crowded city of Calcutta. They brought with them nothing but their desperate problems.

God continued to call Mother Teresa to care for His poor. She had no choice but to return to the Archbishop. Archbishop Perier looked down at the tiny nun. "Do you have any idea what you're asking?" he asked. "Do you have the physical and spiritual strength to carry out your proposed vocation? Do you know what you are demanding of yourself? How will the people accept you? A European woman alone in the slums would not be accepted."

"I am convinced that it is God's work and not my own. He has called me to do His work. I am completely at His disposal. Without Him I can do nothing. With Him all things are possible."

This time the Archbishop advised her to seek the permission of the Mother House of her order. Mother Gertrude, Mother General of the Loreto Sisters, recognized God's voice in Mother Teresa's letter and said, "If God is calling you, I give you my permission with all my heart. I want you to know that we love you. And if you ever want to come back to us there will always be a place for you."

Mother Teresa's request was forwarded to Rome. A nun living and working outside the convent system was unheard of, but she waited, patiently teaching her regular classes and working with the poor. During the ensuing months, Mother Teresa did not forget her quest. But she had every reason to believe the Vatican had.

In September of 1947 Pakistan invaded Kashmir, starting a war between India and Pakistan. This war caused great economic losses to India and fed the religious-nationalistic bitterness with terrible consequences. Many of the poorest were uprooted and forced to travel long distances with little food and water, carrying their sick, their old, their babies. Tempers were short and the country was primed for violence. Whole villages were burned, wives and daughters were raped, some committed suicide.

Surrounded by all this suffering, Mother Teresa felt even more frustrated because her call to help the poorest of the poor was always in her mind, along with the knowledge that she could not begin her mission until the Pope released her from her commitment to the Loreto Sisters.

From the time she was a young girl, Teresa had lung problems, and now it was discovered she indeed had tuberculosis. Her superiors sent her to Asansol, about three hours from Calcutta by train. She taught geography there, worked in the garden and was in charge of the kitchen.

The political situation was confusing and unmanageable, especially in Calcutta, where religious differences were magnified by thousands of refugees.

Trouble broke out in Saint Mary's School between the students and teachers who did not agree on matters. The school authorities were unable to settle the dispute. Archbishop Perier sent for Mother Teresa. She met with the student leaders and within half an hour the problems were solved.

But other problems were in store for Mother Teresa's chosen country. On January 30, 1948 at 5:00 p.m., Mahatama Gandhi was on his way to evening prayer. A Hindu fanatic walked up to him, bowed low, then fired three shots at close range. Gandhi said, "Oh, God," and died.

That same year, on Sunday, August 8th, Father Van Exem celebrated Mass at the Entally Loreto chapel as usual. He told Mother Teresa, "I'd like to speak with you after Mass. Could you meet with me in the convent parlor?" When she entered he said, "Mother Teresa, I have your reply from Rome."

She turned pale and said, "Could I go to the chapel and pray before we read it?"

"Of course."

When she returned from the chapel, he handed her a letter from the Holy Father, Pope Pius XII. Her hands trembled as she read it. It gave her permission to "live alone outside the cloister among the poor of Calcutta with God alone as her protector and guide."

"Can I go to the slums now?" Mother Teresa asked Father Van Exem.

"It is not so simple," he explained. "You are now under obedience to the Archbishop of Calcutta."

He saw the expression of great disappointment flash on her face at the idea of more waiting. "Don't worry," he said. "Your biggest obstacle has been overcome. All you need is a little more patience."

That evening, Mother Teresa came to Father Van Exem in the sacristy of the convent chapel. "Father, I'd like you to bless these for me, please." She held up a very inexpensive white sari, the type poor Bengali women wore, a small cross and a Rosary.

Sister Cenacle, the Mother Superior of Entally where Mother Teresa had lived the last seventeen years, stood next to her, crying. Father Van Exem tried to comfort Sister Cenacle. He told her, "Don't worry, Sister, if this is not God's will, Mother Teresa will return to us in a year."

When Mother Teresa met Archbishop Perier she was relieved to learn that he was now willing to accept that God really was calling her to leave the convent and go serve the poor. "Then am I free to begin, Your Holiness?" she asked.

"Do you know where you will begin?"

"Father Van Exem has suggested I speak to you about going to Patna to the Holy Family Hospital and work with the Medical Mission Sisters so I can learn basic nursing skills."

"That sounds like an excellent idea, Mother Teresa."

That night she wrote the Sisters. On August 15, 1948, she received an invitation to visit the Medical Mission Sisters in Patna. Leaving the Sisters of Loreto was the hardest thing she had ever done. It was even more difficult than leaving her family and her country when she was eighteen years old. She had felt so close to Jesus in this lovely convent and the Sisters had become her family. Everyone at the convent of Loreto loved Mother Teresa and was sad to see her go.

Her pupils wept. "Why couldn't it be another teacher?" they asked. "Why does it have to be Mother Teresa?"

When the time came for her to leave, the girls sang farewell songs in Bengali. Mother Teresa cried with them. Then she went to the chapel for a last prayer. She removed her European habit with its full skirt reaching to the floor, the white coif around the head, and the long black veil. She slipped into her white sari that Father Van Exem had blessed and a plain pair of sandals. As she left the convent grounds, she felt lonelier than she ever had felt in her life. But she knew she was doing God's will and that was all that really mattered. No one saw her as she slipped out the gate in her Indian clothes. She left the warmth of the convent, the spiritual way of life, the friendliness, the encouragement, the organization and loving concern, surrendering herself to God's will with complete trust in His providence.

Once again Mother Teresa was at a train station starting a long journey, but this time there was no mother or sister to say good-bye. She traveled north 240 miles to Patna for a course in practical nursing and hygiene. When she stepped off the train in Patna, an ancient city on the sacred Ganges River, three of the Medical Mission Sisters were there to welcome her and right away she felt at home.

The Holy Family Hospital was staffed by the Medical Mission Sisters who were doctors, nurses, laboratory technicians, and dietitians. Traditionally, the Catholic Church did not allow nuns to do surgery or to deliver babies in their hospitals. Mother Dengel, an Austrian-born woman and head of the Medical Mission Sisters, had obtained permission from the Pope for her Sister-doctors to practice surgery and midwifery, so she could understand Mother Teresa's desire to start new activities and be a nun in a new way.

"I hope to start a new congregation that will live with and be like the poor in India," Mother Teresa told Mother Dengel. "We will wear simple inexpensive saris and sandals, sleep on mattresses on the floor and eat only rice and salt."

"Oh, no, Sister!" Mother Dengel said. "You must not have your Sisters eat only rice and salt. They will all become sick and many will die before they ever get a chance to serve the poor."

"Well, that's just the way it will have to be. I know God wants us to live like the poor, to be one with them. They eat rice and salt and so will we," she insisted.

"You will be committing a serious sin if you have your Sisters work until they are exhausted, expose themselves to the many illnesses of the poor without making certain that they eat the proper food and get the necessary rest. The poor work very little because they have no strength and are often sick. Don't you want your Sisters to be strong and able to labor well for God and His poor?"

"You are right, Mother," Mother Teresa said, realizing Mother Dengel's advice made good sense. "My Sisters will be fed simple food, but they will get enough and it will be nutritious enough to keep them healthy and strong for His work."

The hospital was a converted school building, two stories high. There was a smaller building nearby which housed the operating and delivery room. The Medical Sisters were too busy to spend much time talking with Mother Teresa. They assigned her a cell, a tiny room to sleep in, a chair in the dining and community room, and she was on her own.

Whenever there was an emergency, a new admission, an operation or delivery, Mother Teresa was called at the same time as the doctor. Mother Teresa would come running across the lawn to stay with the patient. While her Bengali was fluent, she had difficulty with Hindi, but she learned rapidly. She always wanted to know what was going on and what she could do to help. She would hold the patient's hand during painful or frightening procedures, console a crying child, and help in any way she could.

The Medical Sisters had many friends in the community and were often invited to weddings, celebrations, wakes for the dead, or thanksgivings for recoveries. Mother Teresa was always happy to go along.

Every evening Mother Teresa would join the Medical Sisters for recreation and they would talk together. When Mother Teresa shared her hopes and ideas with them, they would share their experiences and insights with her. The Medical Sisters had strict regulations about prayer, but prayer time ended at 9:00 p.m. They told Mother Teresa, "Our meals are very simple but we are required to eat enough food and get plenty of protein. We have a daily nap. Everyone has one day of rest with those who have to work on Sunday taking another day off each week."

They wore white cotton habits and veils which were changed at least once a day due to the heat.

One day while Mother Teresa was at the Holy Family Hospital in Patna, she received a visitor who was to play an important part in her work. The visitor, a European woman dressed much like Mother Teresa in a simple sari, found her in the chapel deep in prayer. The woman quietly slipped into the chapel and knelt to thank God for leading her to this unique and courageous nun. She prayed that God would bless her attempts to do His will and use this meeting of two of His servants for the good of His beloved poor. Although the two women had never met before, both had been born in Europe and had answered God's call to render service to the poorest of the poor in India. They had both adopted the Indian habits of dressing, eating, taking their food while sitting on the floor and sleeping on simple mattresses. Both women were always ready to serve anyone in need regardless of caste, religion, sex, or age.

When Mother Teresa got off her knees and prepared to leave the chapel, she was surprised to find that she had company. But she smiled her warm, all-embracing smile and quickly ushered her guest outside the chapel where they could talk without danger of disturbing anyone.

"I'm Jacqueline de Decker," the woman said. "I was born in Belgium, but since the age of seventeen I have longed to give myself entirely to God for the poor of India." Mother Teresa was delighted to meet another soul called by God to serve His poor in the country she loved so much.

"At the beginning, we were a group of eight lay volunteers who shared the same ideal," the woman went on. "But the war separated us. I am a nurse, and during the war I worked with the British troops caring for the wounded. A Jesuit priest asked me to do medical social work in Madras, but on the day of my departure, he died suddenly. The Bishop of Madras advised me to learn the language and customs of India. So I worked in a dispensary and gave instructions. For awhile I also helped with Gandhi's village work."

"Ghandi was a good man," Mother Teresa said.

"Yes," Jacqueline agreed. "He used to call the poorest Indians the children of God. Recently I have been living alone with almost no money and the Indians have accepted me as one of them. They help me with everything I try to do. But the terrible suffering and hopelessness in India will never seem natural to me. I want so much to do something about it, to give myself to God and let Him use me to help in some way."

"With God all things are possible," Mother Teresa said joyfully.

Jacqueline remembered her own feelings of isolation and shock at the enormity of the work. No matter how much she did, it always appeared as nothing compared to the great need that each day became more apparent. She had been advised by friends to seek out Mother Teresa since they seemed to have common goals. Mother Teresa's great love for the poor, her complete trust in God's Providence and her insistence that it was His work they would be doing in Calcutta renewed Jacqueline's strength. The two women became close friends from that first meeting. They worked together at the hospital in Patna and in Mokammeh. In December, Mother Teresa decided to return to Calcutta. She was eager to begin her new mission.

"I wish I could go with you," Jacqueline told her, "but I've been having trouble with my back. The doctors here tell me it's very serious. They feel I must return to Belgium for treatment. As soon as my health is better, I'll join you in Calcutta."

Back in Belgium, however, Jacqueline learned that a diving accident she'd had when she was young had done much more damage than her doctors had originally thought and that she would have to have major surgery. She wrote Mother Teresa, "It will take a little longer than I expected, but with God's help I shall eventually join you in India."

It was the week before Christmas in 1948 that Mother Teresa left Patna for Calcutta. The Medical Sisters gave her a strong pair of sandals as a going-away gift.

Father Van Exem had gone to the superior of the Little Sisters of the Poor in

Calcutta and obtained temporary shelter for Mother Teresa. At St. Joseph's Home, Mother began a short retreat with Father Van Exem, who came to see her each morning. She spent much time praying alone and she helped the Little Sisters care for the elderly each day. Then she began to venture out into the bustees, carrying her lunch since she had no money for food.

Mother Teresa went to visit her old friend, Father Julien Henry, who had worked with her and her Sodality students in the Calcutta bustees. "Do you recognize me?" she asked as he saw her for the first time in her sari. Father Henry pretended not to know her. He kept looking at her as though trying to figure out who she was. "I seem to have seen you before," he said.

"Where is Motijhil?" she asked.

"You should know it well. It is the bustee on the other side of your convent wall."

They both laughed.

That day Mother Teresa started an open-air school in Motijhil. She had five pupils the first day, all in their teens, but none of them had ever been to school. Since she had no blackboard, she used a stick and wrote the Bengali alphabet on the ground. At noon, she gave the students milk and in the evening she gave them soap as prizes. Most of them were so poor they had never even seen a bar of soap before and were overjoyed with such luxury. She got water and showed them how to use the soap to clean themselves.

The next day, a few girls from St. Mary's School came to help her. When she started the work, Mother Teresa had only 5 rupees (about 70 cents). But as people came to know what she was doing, they brought her money and supplies.

She was teaching the alphabet to children who would probably never become literate or have a book to read, teaching them to use soap when they probably would never be able to afford to buy it. At times she felt lost and useless. God had pulled her out of the convent where she was useful. Exactly what was He calling her to do? She felt completely inadequate for this new mission. But God had called her and she knew that He would give her everything she needed to do His work. She clung to Him, surrendered herself completely.

Little by little He led her where He wanted her to go, showing her what He wanted her to do.

One day as she was walking home from the bustees, a priest came up to her. He asked her for a contribution for his work. Mother Teresa had left home with only a few rupees and had given all but one to the poor. She gave her last rupee to the priest. That afternoon, the same priest came to see her. He brought an envelope. "A man gave me this envelope because he had heard about your projects with the poor and he wanted to help." Mother Teresa opened the envelope and found 50 rupees. "I had the feeling at that moment that God had blessed the work and would never abandon me," she recalled later on.

Missionaries of Charity

One day Father Henry received a phone call from Michael Gomes, one of his parishioners. "Please come and bring the Last Sacraments, Father. My mother is very ill. She may be dying." After giving Mrs. Gomes the Last Rites, Father Henry began telling Michael about Mother Teresa and her work. "Do you know of a small room, a hut, or something like that around here, where Mother Teresa could begin her work with the poor?"

Michael's eight-year-old daughter immediately said, "The whole upstairs is empty. She could live here."

"That's right," Michael Gomes said. "Do you want to see it?" He took Father Henry on a tour of the old mansion. Then he asked, "Well, Father, do you think she could use this space?"

"I don't know," Father Henry said. "It's much better than she was looking for. She wants to live the same way the very poorest people live."

"But she is a nun," Michael said. "She should live in a nice place."

"Thank you very much for your offer," Father Henry said. "I will tell Mother Teresa about it."

When Mother Teresa saw the place, she said, "Thank you so much, but this place is too nice and too big." But after a long desperate search, she decided to accept one of the upstairs rooms in Michael Gomes' home. It was early in 1949 when Mother Teresa arrived at the Gomes' house carrying all of her belongings in an old suitcase. Her friend, Ma Charu, the old cook from St. Mary's school, was with her. They had one piece of furniture with them, a kitchen chair.

Michael Gomes refused to accept any money for rent or food. "You are doing God's work," he said. "Let this be my contribution to Him."

Father Henry gave her a corner at a nearby church for an outdoor dispensary. She asked Michael Gomes if he knew anyone who could get her some medicine. "We have a dispensary. Now we need something to dispense."

"I know of someone who might give you some medicine," Michael told her. "It's a man I've never met but we have spoken on the phone many times." Michael and Mother Teresa went to a big shop with the list of medicines she wanted. The manager was very busy but because their order was so large, he waited on them himself. When he told her the price, Mother said, "Since these are for the poorest of the poor, I would like to have them for free."

He could not believe his ears. "You have come to the wrong place, Lady," he said. "Let me finish my work in peace."

Mother Teresa sat right down and said her Rosary. Michael Gomes sat next to her. When Mother Teresa finished her Rosary, she stood up to go. Having had a change of heart, the manager brought her three parcels. "Here is all the medicine you had on your list. You may have it as a gift from the company."

"God will bless you for taking care of His children," Mother Teresa told the man.

In the streets, Mother Teresa was followed by beggars. Starving orphans called out, "No father! No mother! Give money! Give food!" People with one eye, one leg, lepers, living skeletons, followed her pointing their fingers to their mouths to show that they were hungry. Some were naked. Many were unable to walk. Some followed her on their hands and knees. Her heart went out to all of them. She moved towards those stretched out on the pavement, too ill to move. Sometimes it was impossible to tell whether they were alive or dead without touching them.

Before she had any Sisters to help her, Mother Teresa would take Michael Gomes' young daughter or his niece with her. They would leave the house early in the morning and return for lunch. One day they came home very late and Mrs. Gomes was terribly worried. There was a bad storm and she was afraid something had happened to them. When they entered the house, Mother Teresa was drenched but she said only, "I'm so sorry the girls got wet."

She told how they had found a woman with a child in a broken-down hut. The child was dying with a high fever. The woman was standing in water above her knees, holding a broken enamel bowl over her child's head. Because she was unable to pay the eight rupees rent for that miserable room, the landlord sent his men to tear down the roof and drive the poor woman and her sick child out into the pouring rain. Mother Teresa sighed. "I must go back at once and see what we can do. That child has a fever of 104 degrees. Just for eight rupees the child is dying in the rain and whatever few things they have are floating on the water."

The next day, Mother Teresa went searching for a home for her homeless dying. She walked until her legs and feet ached. That night she wrote in her diary: "How exhausted the really poor must get, walking around in search of food or medicine. I have been really tempted by the thought of the comfortable life of the Loreto Convent. My God, because of my free choice and for love of You alone, I am going to stay here and do whatever Your will demands of me."

Seeing the urgency of the situation, Mother Teresa prayed for help. She wanted other Sisters eager to commit themselves to serving Christ in His poor.

Unable to find a home for her abandoned dying, Mother Teresa began bringing them home with her to the Gomes' house. She washed the babies who were always filthy since their families could not afford soap, and water was difficult to come by. For many of the babies, this was the first bath of their lives.

One morning, a beautiful young Bengali girl in an elegant sari knocked at the door. She was Subhasini Das, one of Mother Teresa's former students. Subhasini had a smooth, dark, flawless complexion, luxurious black hair, a radiant smile and sparkling brown eyes. Mother Teresa was surprised to see her. They stood smiling at one another for several seconds. Then Subhasini said, "Mother Teresa, I have come to live with you and help with the work." Mother Teresa took Subhasini's hands in hers and felt how smooth and soft they were. "Look at my hands," she told the girl. "See how red and rough they are. And look at my clothes. You would have to give up your beautiful saris." She led Subhasini up the stairs to the upper room where she was living and showed her the poor who were sharing the room with her. "Religious life, especially this kind of religious life, demands great self-sacrifice," Mother Teresa told her. "A nun has to forget herself completely and dedicate herself to God and neighbor."

"I understand," the girl said. "I have thought about nothing else for a long time. I'm ready. I beg you to accept me."

Mother Teresa looked at her carefully. The qualities she wanted in her future missionaries were healthy mind and body, ability to learn, common sense, natural joy and unfailing good humor. She saw all of these in Subhasini. "Come and see me again on Saint Joseph's day," Mother Teresa said. It was a difficult thing to do, to send away her first recruit, but she had to test her vocation.

On St. Joseph's day, March 19, 1949, Mother Teresa was praying in the chapel when a knock sounded at the door. When she opened it, she found Subhasini standing there, wearing a simple sari and no makeup or jewelry.

"I am ready to give myself completely to God's work."

Mother Teresa now handed her a cheap cotton sari like the one she herself was wearing. Subhasini put it on immediately. "What name have you chosen for your new life?" Mother Teresa asked her. "If it is all right with you, Mother, I should like to be Sister Agnes."

Mother Teresa was touched by this loving gesture. "Welcome to your new home, Sister Agnes," she said. "Let's go into the chapel now and thank Our Lady and Jesus for sending me my first spiritual daughter."

One month later, along came Magdalena Gomes (not related to Michael

Gomes), another former student from St. Mary's, who was enrolled in the University. She took the name Sister Gertrude. Mother Teresa needed a doctor badly and she wanted Sister Gertrude to take the Bachelor of Medicine curriculum, but Sister Gertrude was having difficulty with the required mathematics course. Mother gave her a crash course on the subject, and the Sister was able to pass the examination and become a doctor.

Then came Sister Dorothy, another graduate of St. Mary's who came to work with her former teacher.

Another former student, Sister Margaret Mary, came from East Pakistan and did not know any English. Mother had her speaking the language in a few months.

Also among the first to join Mother Teresa was Agnes Vincent, from a well-to-do Bengali family. When she was in the tenth grade, Mother Teresa had taken her to the Motijihl bustee. As Agnes walked with Mother Teresa through the over-crowded, filthy slums, Mother had explained how important it was that someone should care for these poor, neglected people. And by God's graces, Agnes Vincent had come to help Mother Teresa care for those poor people who had haunted her mind ever since that first visit. Agnes became Sister Florence.

Beatrice Rosario came to join Mother in the bustees although her family strongly opposed the idea. During those days, girls in India had almost no freedom to make their own decisions and going into the bustees to work with the poor was completely unheard of. The Sisters were working with people neither valued nor respected by society. Beatrice's family could not understand how she could give her life to work with the poorest, with lepers and the homeless. But she had heard God's call and she became Sister Bernard. Beatrice was joining on faith alone.

The first nine girls who joined Mother were all former students. Together they went from door to door asking for help. They then took the food they had been given to those who were starving.

The Sisters taught the children in the bustees to love God and their neighbors, and to respect the dignity of human life. They knew they were answering God's call to see Him in the least of His children. "Whatever you do for the least of my people, you do for me."

Michael Gomes watched with joy as his upper floor became a real convent. He was a very religious man and loved having so much prayer in his home.

All the Sisters wore the plain white cotton sari with a blue border and a crucifix held on with a safety pin. They all cut their hair. One young Sister was laughing as they cut off her lovely long hair. "It feels like Jesus is playing with my curls," she said as she stood in the breeze, most of her hair on the ground covering her bare feet.

She and her first twelve girls got up at 5:30 every morning. They prayed and attended Mass and by 7:30 they were out in the bustees.

Other helpers came to join in the work. Doctors and nurses volunteered their services. The Community continued to grow. Most of the novices were middle-class Indian girls. Some came from rich upper classes and there were some Anglo-Indians.

One day, one of the Sisters came down with the chicken-pox and had to be segregated from the others. Mother asked Michael Gomes if she could use another room. "Of course, Mother. They are all at your disposal." Slowly, Mother's Sisters began to take over the entire upper floor. There was a problem with bathing, however, as there were now thirty Sisters and only two bathrooms. Then one day some builders from St. Teresa's parish came with bricks and bamboo matting and put bathing cubicles on the roof.

The Sisters enjoyed themselves so much, the Gomes family could hear their laughter all over the house. The girls would run and play hop-scotch and tug-of-war. But they had a discipline, a bell system. When the bell rang, they would stop whatever they were doing and pray. Another bell rang when it was time to eat. And still another when it was time to go out. There was no regular schedule for work. As they saw a need, they did all they could to alleviate it.

Many of the Sisters were still going to school. Mother tutored them and encouraged them to continue with their studies.

Mother Teresa insisted that the Sisters go to bed early, but she herself wrote letters, made plans and worked on her order's Constitution late into the night.

"I've chosen the name Missionaries of Charity," she told her Sisters, "because we are carriers of God's love." She was convinced that if they were to understand, love, and serve the poorest, they would have to live like them. "Our only possessions will be two cotton saris, underwear, sandals, a crucifix, a metal bucket for washing and a straw mat for our bed. Then we will be ready to go anywhere we are needed."

"We will not attempt to convert people of other faiths to Christianity or other Christians to Catholicism," Mother told them. "We will see every human being as Christ, and we will help Hindus to be better Hindus, Muslims to be better Muslims and Christians to be better Christians, by helping them to come closer to God." In their daily work, the Sisters lived the Mass by touching Jesus in the broken bodies of the poor and feeding Him in the starving people. "This is all Jesus told us," Mother said. "Love one another as I have loved you."

Father Henry and some of the boys from his parish built a wooden altar and candlesticks for the Sisters' chapel. Father Van Exem gave Mother a picture of the Immaculate Heart of Mary which she hung above the altar.

Above the altar were the words: I THIRST. Mother Teresa said to her Sisters, "'I thirst' is something much deeper than Jesus just saying 'I love you.' Until you know deep inside that Jesus thirsts for you, you can't begin to know who He wants to be for you. Or who He wants you to be for Him."

The Sisters referred to their home as the "Upper Room" since it was on the second floor of the Gomes' house and it resembled the upper room where Christ and His apostles ate the Last supper.

The Sisters were closely united and keenly felt their oneness in the Lord. They prayed, studied, slept, ate, talked, sang, played, cooked, washed clothes, scrubbed floors, repaired clothes, and made bandages together. English was the language of the community, and those who didn't know English were given lessons. Mother Teresa instructed them and showed them by her example how to surrender themselves completely to their Lord.

Father Henry and Father Van Exem helped Mother Teresa prepare her Constitution to be presented to the Holy Father in Rome. On October 7, 1950, the Feast of the Most Holy Rosary, Archbishop Perier and Father Van Exem came to the Gomes' home to say Mass in the little chapel. Father Van Exem read the letter from Rome declaring the Missionaries of Charity an official church organization. Mother Teresa and her Sisters were overjoyed. They were now official. The fact that this wonderful news came on the Feast of the Rosary was even more meaningful for Mother Teresa, since she loved the Blessed Mother and the Rosary dedicated to her.

Every morning they went to the bustees as before. They opened more schools. If they had to go a long distance, they took the cramped, suffocating trams or buses used by the common people. They prayed their Rosaries as they traveled. When Mother asked, "How far did you go?" the Sisters would answer, "Two Rosaries," or "Three Rosaries," depending on where they had gone.

One evening when Mother Teresa was returning home, Michael Gomes called her. "Mother, you remember my niece, Agnes, who used to go with you and Mabel to visit the bustees when you first came to live here?"

"Of course I remember little Agnes. She always said she wanted to live with me and give her whole life to the poor."

"Well, Agnes is in Holy Family Hospital in Patna where you studied nursing. She has tuberculosis and it looks like she may be dying."

"Let's go in the chapel and pray for her," Mother Teresa said with great sadness.

Michael said, "There is only one thing Agnes wants in all the world . . . to be a Missionary of Charity and give herself to Jesus in the poorest of the poor."

"But she is so ill," Mother said.

"Isn't there any way she could take vows? It would give her such joy."

"Let's go speak with the Archbishop," Mother suggested and the two set off to visit Archbishop Perier after some prayer time in the chapel.

The Archbishop of Calcutta gave special permission for Agnes to enter the order.

A short time later, Mother Teresa and Agnes' father went to Patna. The Medical Missionary Sisters were delighted to see Mother again. When she told them the purpose of her visit, they said, "We are so glad you've come. In spite of all her pain, Agnes stays cheerful and friendly. She always has a smile. Everyone loves her and wants to do something for her. But all she wants is to join the Missionaries of Charity. Of course there is no hope that she will recover unless Our Dear Lord should grant us a miracle."

On October 3, 1952, a few days before Agnes' twentieth birthday, Mother Teresa and Agnes' father joined the young girl in her room in Holy Family Hospital. Agnes was very thin and very pale, but her happiness created a glow about her. She took the vows of poverty, obedience, chastity, and the fourth vow of free service to the poorest of the poor.

"What name have you chosen, Agnes, to signify the beginning of your new life?" Mother asked.

"I will be Sister Maria Goretti, Mother."

Mother Teresa thought it was appropriate for Agnes to choose for her patron a recently canonized Italian teenager who had been stabbed to death defending her virginity. She had chosen a saint who was close to her age.

"Now, Sister Maria Goretti, you are officially part of the Missionaries of Charity and all your prayers and sufferings will enable us active missionaries to do beautiful things for Jesus because of you."

"I never thought I could ever be so happy," Sister Maria Goretti told Mother.

"It is your wedding day," Mother said.

Since their first meeting in 1948 in Patna, Mother Teresa and Jacqueline de Decker had carried on spirited correspondence. The heat and discomfort of India had caused Jacqueline much pain and aggravated her injured back. Jacqueline too had wanted to join Mother Teresa's order. She would have been the first recruit, but God had other plans for her. She had gone to Belgium for an operation, expecting to return to Calcutta to work with Mother. But her arms, one of her eyes, and her right leg became paralyzed. The doctors determined that the only way she could avoid complete paralysis was to undergo a number of operations. When Jacqueline realized that she could never return to India to work, she became very depressed. But gradually she surrendered herself to God's will.

In the autumn of 1952, Mother Teresa wrote to Jacqueline: "Today I am going to propose something to you. Why not become spiritually bound to our society which you love so dearly? While we work in the slums, you share in the merit, the prayers and the work. I need souls like yours to pray and suffer for the work. You will be in body in Belgium, but in soul in India. Be brave and cheerful and offer much that we may bring many souls to God."

For the first time, Jacqueline realized that God was not rejecting her but giving her a special role in His work. She felt a burden lift. Her heart became joyful. She sat down immediately and wrote Mother Teresa that she was eager to become spiritually united with the Missionaries of Charity.

That Christmas, Sister Maria Goretti wanted her Uncle, Michael Gomes, to spend the holidays with her. When he arrived in Patna, the Mother Superior of the Medical Missionaries told him, "The doctors can't understand how your niece is staying alive. Both of her lungs have been eaten away." When he saw his niece, Michael was shocked at how thin and pale she was. But as soon as she recognized him, her beautiful smile lit up her face.

"Hello, Sister Maria Goretti," he said.

"I'm a Missionary of Charity now," she said proudly. "Now my suffering has a purpose. It goes to save souls, Uncle Michael. Isn't that beautiful? As sick as I am, I can do something that matters. Nothing is more important than saving souls."

Nirmal Hriday

It was 1952, and Mother Teresa searched the teeming streets of Calcutta for those in need of her help. She appeared older than her forty-two years with her back already bent and her face weathered, but she still had the energy of a young athlete. Although she continually fingered her beads saying the Rosary, she was ever alert for someone in trouble, eager to serve God in the poor with total abandonment.

Spotting an old woman lying in a pile of rubbish, Mother Teresa rushed to her side to hear her say, "To think my own son put me here!" Upon closer observation, Mother saw that the woman was half eaten by rats and ants. She looked more dead than alive. Making the Sign of the Cross with chapped hands that had known much hard work, Mother picked up the dying woman and carried her to the nearest hospital.

Death and dying were common in the streets of Calcutta. Just as citizens of other nations watch news reports of death and violence without a tear or prayer, the wealthier Indians closed their eyes to the tragic reality around them. But Mother Teresa, who saw Jesus in every human being, could never turn her back on the dying Christ.

At the hospital, a receptionist said, "We can't admit this woman. We have room only for curable patients. She is beyond hope."

Struggling to see Jesus in this bureaucrat who had apparently become anesthetized to suffering, Mother fought to control her temper. "I won't move from here until you admit her," she said evenly with a steadfast gaze.

Only a few weeks earlier, a naked beggar boy about thirteen years old lay dying by the roadside in a residential neighborhood. The owner of a nearby home called an ambulance and had the boy taken to the hospital. Since he was homeless, naked, and apparently near death, the hospital had refused to accept him and sent him back to the spot where he had been found. He died alone in the gutter. However, the Calcutta newspapers picked up the story, and people who themselves had stepped over dying bodies wept when they read it.

Not wanting any more unfavorable publicity, the hospital administration decided to admit the woman Mother Teresa had brought them. The receptionist whispered to a nurse, then returned to Mother Teresa. "If you insist, we'll take her in. But I want you to know you are robbing someone else of a bed, someone we might have saved." Mother Teresa took a seat in the corner of the waiting room and began praying her Rosary for the poor woman.

Soon the receptionist told her, "The woman died." There was no emotion in her voice. Mother walked away, determined to change the fate of such forgotten people. "Cats and dogs are treated better than this," she said sadly.

Going straight to the Calcutta Health Department, she pleaded for an end to such horrible neglect. "Give me a place where these people can die with love and dignity. It is a shame before the world that people die like animals on our city streets." One of the city officials said, "She's got a point. There's been a whole series of newspaper articles showing people dying in the streets. Something must be done." Many of the officials had already heard of Mother's Missionaries of Charity and their helpers in the bustees. All of them were disturbed by the media's criticism and they realized that this newcomer with an iron will and direct manner was offering to care for the starving, dying, homeless, perhaps solving a serious problem facing their city. They huddled together talking all at once while Mother calmly said her Rosary, asking Jesus' Mother to give her a home for the destitute dying.

"Mother," one of the men said finally, "you have a choice between two buildings. One is next door to your convent. The other used to be a pilgrims' rest home next door to the temple of Kali, the Hindu goddess of death and destruction."

"I'd like to see the old rest home," Mother said immediately.

"Wouldn't the other building be more convenient, Mother?" the man asked.

"The rest home is a sacred spot to the Indians," Mother said. "They would feel close to God there, and that's more important than our convenience. It's Jesus we are taking care of in the homeless and He never worried about whether dying for us on the cross was convenient."

The health officials took Mother Teresa to the Kali temple and showed her the ancient pilgrims' hostel. She stood looking at the dusty old building, empty except for a small crowd of rowdy men gathered around an old dark man with one arm who was drinking from a dirty bottle. There were two great rooms at right angles to each other, joined by a passage. The building was many hundreds of years old. A strong musty odor permeated the air. The only windows were small and placed high on the thick walls, not permitting much sunlight. There was a beautiful stream of light near Mother. She imagined the two rooms filled with dying people lovingly cared for by her Missionaries of Charity.

"This will be the best place for Indian people to rest before they go home to heaven," she said. "Yes, this is the building I want."

"But Mother," one of the health officials said, "you haven't even looked at the other building."

"There is no need," she said emphatically.

"When would you like to open?" the man asked.

"Tomorrow," she replied promptly.

Mother Teresa knelt on the hard, dirty floor to thank God and Our Lady. Then she hurried home to share the good news with the Sisters. They stopped everything they were doing to welcome their beloved Mother Teresa home, and they all gathered around her for a blessing. Then they went into the little chapel to thank God for the wonderful news Mother had just given them, and to ask His help in their new home for the dying.

After prayers and a small meal, they gathered cleaning utensils and rushed to the hostel. They set to work immediately scrubbing floors, washing the filthy walls, dusting, moving in mats and doing everything they could to make the place clean and comfortable. Working late into the night, they were exhausted but joyful when they finally finished their preparations.

"We'll name our home Nirmal Hriday, the place of the Immaculate Heart of Mary, since it was Jesus' Mother who found it for us," Mother said.

Just as she had promised, the next morning they were ready for their first patient. It was a woman found lying outside the same hospital to which Mother had taken the old woman whose son had thrown her out with his garbage. It did not take them long to fill the house with dying people.

For the first few months, Mother and her Sisters had a difficult time. The Brahmin priests who conducted the worship of Kali in the temple did not like having Roman Catholic Sisters next door. They spied on her. Rumors spread that she was trying to convert the Hindu people to Christianity when in truth she allowed each person to die with rituals of his or her own religion, be it Muslim, Hindu, Buddhist, Catholic, Protestant, Jewish, or any other. The Hindu priests said, "She is bribing them with a place to die in."

Before they had enough evidence to go the local Congress Committee, a group of young Hindu men who believed the rumors took it upon themselves to get Mother Teresa and her Sisters out of the pilgrim's rest home.

"Get out!" they shouted. "You don't belong here!" and they even threw stones. One of their stones just missed hitting a dying woman. Mother decided to go to the source of the problem, the head of the Brahmin priests in the Kali temple next door.

"Here I am," she told him. "Kill me right now if you wish. But please don't harm the dying."

One of his spies had already informed him of Mother's good work. He went to see for himself. "Far from profaning the goddess Kali, this woman seems like the goddess herself," he told them. "Do not harm her in any way." What he had seen in person was enough to convince him that she was indeed an asset and not a liability to the temple. From that day on they were friends.

The young men who had been throwing stones now decided it was completely up to them to go to the local Congress Committee to have Mother and her Sisters removed. The Committee in turn went to the Police Commissioner saying, "This foreign woman is forcing our poor people to become Christians right next to the temple of Kali. It's a disgrace and it must be stopped."

"I'll get her out of Kali's house," he promised. "But first I want to see the situation for myself."

When he arrived at the home, Mother Teresa was taking care of a dying patient. She was putting medicine on an open wound covered with wriggling maggots. There was a terrible odor in the room, but Mother did not seem to notice. She looked up when the Commissioner entered and asked, "Is there something I can do for you?"

"No, thank you," he said. "I just want to look around."

"I'll be happy to escort you," Mother told him.

"No, thank you. I'll see things for myself." Mother returned to caring for the dying man.

The Commissioner walked through the passage and into the next room. In the meantime, the young boys came in to watch Mother. When the Commissioner returned to the men's side of the house, he told the boys, "I gave you my word I would put this lady out and I will keep my word. But before I do, you must get your mothers and your sisters to do the work she is doing. Only then will I exercise my authority against her." He led the boys to the big stone image of the goddess Kali that was behind the building. "Here's a statue of the Kali you worship," he told them. Then he brought them back to see Mother Teresa who was still treating the dying man. "Here is the living Kali," he said. "How can we throw her out?" Realizing they had been defeated, the boys left the home. After that, the Police Commissioner always tried to protect Mother and her Nirmal Hriday.

One day, a young novice was trying to clean a wound with a pair of tweezers. She held them at arm's length trying to keep from touching the open wound, which was oozing with pus. Mother Teresa noticed her and rushed to her side. Mother bent her face almost to the wound without seeming to notice the strong distressing odor.

She told the young girl, "You have to realize that this is Jesus. We are cleansing His wounds. We could not do this work if we did not believe it was the body of

Christ we are taking care of."

A priest arrived to say Mass in the home for the dying. The Sisters helped him to prepare the medicine table on the platform of the men's section for his altar. Although there were only six Christian patients, there was silence and great respect for the service. As the priest began saying the Mass, a man was brought in on the verge of death. He was in great pain and could not stop moaning. The Sisters had to go right up on the platform to get the injection to ease his pain. Another man cried out in pain and Mother Teresa went to give him comfort. She held him tenderly in her arms. The priest continued saying the Mass.

One day, Mother found a crowd on the pavement outside the Kali Temple. In their midst was a man lying in his own mess. No one wanted to touch him because he was in the last stages of cholera, a very infectious disease. Mother came closer to him and saw that he was one of the Brahmin priests. Gently, she picked him up and carried him into the house where she and the Sisters took care of him. The Hindu priest was delirious and so ill he blasphemed against God for putting him into this terrible condition. The other priests came to visit him and were saddened by his unhappy state. Mother and the Sisters prayed often for him and touched his hand or forehead each time they passed him.

One morning Mother Teresa was making her rounds, speaking to each patient in Hindi or Bengali.

"How are you today?"

"You are looking much better."

"Are you eating?"

She came to a very young man who was close to death. A young Sister was rubbing his forehead as he moaned in pain.

Mother Teresa reached down, straightened his head on the pillow and asked the Sister, "Does he have any family?"

"No, Mother."

"Does anyone know he's here?" Mother asked then.

"He has no one, Mother."

Mother shook her head sadly. "He's so young." She touched him gently, then continued on her rounds.

Before she left for the day, Mother returned to the young man. "How is he, Sister?" she asked.

"Well, he's dying, Mother," the Sister said.

Mother Teresa bent down and looked at his face. "So peaceful," she said. "He's going home to Jesus."

Being surrounded by so much love and concern, even the Hindu priest with cholera began to change his attitude. He stopped cursing God and began to speak calmly. He smiled at the Sisters and thanked them for the many kindnesses they were showing him. When the other priests from the temple came to visit him, they were astonished at how much he had changed.

One day, he called Mother Teresa and said, "Please give me your blessing, Mother." She wet his lips with water from the Ganges River, a sacred ritual for the Hindus. "God bless you, my friend," she said softly. "You are going home to God."

The man smiled weakly. "Thank you, Mother Teresa," he said. Then he closed his eyes and died.

One of the Sisters touched him gently. "Just think, Mother. He is seeing the face of God." Mother did not answer. Her attention was fixed completely on the face of the Hindu priest. She was seeing Christ in His Mother's arms after He was taken down from the cross. She reached out and lovingly touched his bare feet, then covered him and said, "It is finished."

Shishu Bhavan

"You can do more from your bed of pain than I running on my feet," Mother wrote to Jacqueline de Decker in January 1953, explaining her ideas for the Sick and Suffering Links.

"Anyone who wishes to become a Missionary of Charity, a carrier of God's love, is welcome. But I want especially the paralyzed, the crippled, the incurables to join for they will bring many souls to the feet of Jesus. Each Sister will have a second self, a person whose prayers and sufferings are offered for her. One thing we must all have in common is total surrender to God, loving trust and perfect cheerfulness."

Mother Teresa gave Jacqueline the names of her novices. The first ten would be professed on April 12, 1953, and Mother wanted a Sick and Suffering partner for each of them. When Jacqueline received Mother Teresa's letter, she was in the hospital recovering from her thirtieth operation. She soon found enough patients willing to offer their pain and prayers to give each Sister a suffering second self.

Mother Teresa wrote to her suffering spiritual children: "Our Lord must love you very much to give you so great a part in His suffering. You are His chosen ones. Be brave and cheerful and offer much for us that we may bring many souls to God."

Now that the Missionaries of Charity were a recognized Diocesan congregation, they were being blessed with many vocations. They occupied the entire upper floor of the Gomes' house on Creek Lane and were sleeping side-by-side like sardines, praying for a permanent house.

Mother was offered a small dilapidated house that appeared ready to collapse. When she pointed this out to the man who was showing the Sisters around, he jumped up and down to demonstrate the sturdiness and promptly disappeared through the floor in a splintering of wood and clouds of dust.

Mother made a novena to St. Cecilia.

A wealthy Muslim decided to move to Pakistan and put his house up for sale. It was on the same street as St. Teresa's Church where Father Julien Henry had ministered to the Bengali community since 1938. As soon as he heard about this big house for sale, the priest went to see the Muslim gentleman. The property actually consisted of three houses with a courtyard. It was at 54A Lower Circular Road, in the heart of Calcutta. The streets were noisy, crowded with pedestrians, streetcars, vendors, children at play, people rushing to work. The Muslim gentleman greeted Father Henry with great enthusiasm. "I love you, Father. I studied with the Jesuits at St. Xavier's. I have always loved priests." He showed Father Henry the houses.

Father told him about Mother Teresa and her work and asked, "How much do you want for the place?" Father Henry asked.

"To you I will sell it for 7,500 rupees, less than the price I paid for the land."

At the time, the Archbishop was being operated on for cataracts, but Father Henry went to him and explained the urgency. Within three days they had the house. When Father Henry took Mother Teresa to see the place, she said, "Father, it is much too big. What will we do with all this?" Father Henry smiled. "Mother, you will need it all. There will be a day when you will ask where to put all of your people." Thus began the Mother House.

Sister Maria Goretti, Michael Gomes' little niece, died on September 8, 1953, and was buried in Patna near Holy Family Hospital where she had spent the last year of her life. "Now we have a Missionary of Charity in heaven," Mother Teresa said. She was convinced that with a Sister in heaven, the Sick and Suffering Sisters could do more to help the active Sisters save souls.

She wrote to Jacqueline: "There is nothing special for you to do, but allow Jesus to live His life in you by accepting whatever He gives and by giving whatever He takes with a smile."

In 1954, Mother Teresa met a woman who was destined to co-found a lay organization to assist the Missionaries of Charity in creating a bond of love encircling the entire world. Ann Blaikie, a British citizen living with her husband and two children in Calcutta, was expecting another baby. She was no longer able to work full time in the Good Companion Shop where she and her friends sold crafts made by poor people. Her servants took care of the children while she sat on her balcony wondering how to help those in need and keep herself busy until the new baby arrived.

She thought about Mother Teresa. She had never met her, but she had read articles about her work in the newspapers, and her friend, Margaret McKenzie, had mentioned Mother Teresa several times. Ann contacted her friend, who was also pregnant, and they went together to see Mother, who took them to Nirmal Hriday, the home for the dying. On the way, Ann and her friend offered to collect toys for Mother's annual Christmas party that they had read about in the newspaper. Mother immediately accepted their offer. Then she said, "Could you raise enough money to buy dresses, shirts and shoes for all our Christian children at Christmas?"

Ann found a dozen friends, other European and American women living in Calcutta. They made angels from tin foil and beads, and sold them to raise money to buy the clothes Mother wanted. They collected old toys that they carefully repaired and painted.

After the Christmas party, Mother Teresa came to thank the women for the wonderful job they had done. Then she asked them, "Now could you help with clothes and presents for the Muslim children's annual festival?" After that, there was the Hindu children's party.

It became obvious that there was a year-round need for them. The group called themselves the Marian Society and grew larger. Indians and Anglo-Indians joined them. Many of the helpers lived in big beautiful homes with servants and many luxuries. It was hard for them to imagine the lives of the very poor. Although they were surrounded with poverty, they didn't see it until they began working with Mother. Visiting Nirmal Hriday, they came face to face with the very poor and their suffering. They saw the pain around them and their lives changed. They could recognize the poor as their sisters and brothers, and they became more sensitive to their needs.

Mother Teresa and two members of the Marian Society found a newborn baby being dragged down the street in a dog's mouth. Tenderly, Mother took the baby and brought it home. The baby died shortly afterwards, but at least it had known a few moments of love in its short, sad life. They found babies in garbage bins, in gutters, on doorsteps, or in churches where their own mothers had put them because they were unable to feed the children they already had and didn't know where to get help. More and more children were being born to mothers unable to care for them. Some of these poor babies were brought to Mother Teresa by the midwives who delivered them. Mother Teresa was looking for a house for these children. She was considering a certain building, but felt it might cost too much.

She told Michael Gomes, "A lady asked me to pray for her husband to quit drinking. He drinks a whole bottle of whiskey every day. Well, if he can spend that much money every day buying something that is bad for his health, I can spend a part of that money to rent a children's home."

Mr. Gomes looked at Mother questioningly, "I can't understand what you are saying, Mother," he said. "What does the price of a bottle of whiskey have to do with whether or not you should rent a home for children?"

"You're a man," Mother Teresa told him. "Men make their decisions based on what sounds reasonable. Women listen to their hearts. And when we do follow our hearts, we are usually right."

"You are right about that, Mother," Mr. Gomes said. "Love is more often right than is reason."

In 1955, she opened her first children's home, Shishu Bhavan. She wanted to give love and care to all unwanted children who would otherwise have to care for themselves or die alone in the streets. Shishu Bhavan was a plain two-storied building, a few blocks from the Mother House. There was a high gray wall in front of the building with a green iron gate for cars and a small brown door for people who were on foot. In the large open courtyard, the Sisters placed a huge statue of Our Lady. It was not long before children played everywhere. The walls were soon covered with drawings and children's names scrawled in their own handwriting. Inside the main building was a room for premature infants, many of them victims of attempted abortions. There was a long row of cribs. Each new baby was washed, fed, given whatever medicine it needed, and dressed. The Sisters wrapped them in colorful blankets knitted or quilted by helpers from the Marian Society. The babies wore tiny booties small enough for little dolls.

"Never refuse any child a home," Mother told her Sisters and helpers. "Remember each child is the Baby Jesus." So, even if it meant the babies had to sleep three or more in a crib, the Sisters always made room for one more.

Sometimes people who died in Nirmal Hriday had no one to care for their children. Babies were often left on the doorstep of the Mother House or the children's home. Parents would bring their children and say, "Mother, please take care of them. We have no food and they are sick." The police, social workers and doctors all sent children who needed homes to Mother. "Just as Our Lady and St. Joseph made a beautiful home for Jesus in Nazareth, we must provide a loving home for these children."

Many of the children were dying. Some were in the last stages of tuberculosis while others were starving. Many of them were victims of abortion, too tiny to live. Often their stomachs stuck out and their little arms and legs were like sticks. Many were so small that their lives were miraculous, a special gift from God. Mother Teresa would hand a tiny baby to a Sister or a helper. "Hold her and let her know a little human love before she goes home to her Father."

Often the babies died soon after their arrival. "I don't care what people say about how many of our babies die," Mother said. "We have to let them come to us. These babies must not die uncared for and unloved. Even a tiny baby can feel. If they are going to die, they must die beautifully, knowing all the love we can give them." Only half of the tiniest babies lived. Usually the Sisters spent a whole week taking care of a baby before it smiled for the first time. Shishu Bhavan had enough space for 100 children at a time. Mother Teresa kept teenage girls at Shishu Bhavan, but sent older boys to a Boy's Town run by the Catholic Church in a nearby village.

A little boy, whose parents had both died, refused to eat anything and would not talk or play with anyone. Mother Teresa noticed that he would smile whenever a certain Sister came near him. So she let that Sister take care of him while someone else did her work. The little boy began to eat all his meals and to play with the other children.

One day Mother Teresa picked up a little girl in a Calcutta street. The child was about six years old and all alone. Mother could tell by looking at her that she hadn't eaten for several days. So Mother gave her a crust of bread. The little girl started to eat slowly, one crumb at a time. "Eat the bread," Mother Teresa told the child. "Go on, eat it."

The little girl said, "I'm afraid to eat it all. When the bread is finished, I will be hungry all over again."

"No," Mother Teresa promised, "We will make sure you have food."

Once Mother took an entire family of six children to raise. The father had disappeared, leaving his wife and children with nothing. The mother had managed to keep all the children alive until she herself died from starvation. For an entire day, the children did not know what to do with their mother's body. Finally the neighbors took care of the body, but they were too poor to continue taking care of the children. Rita, the oldest girl, who was fourteen years old, was determined to keep the family together, but she was afraid the baby would die because he just lay on the bed, not moving, not even making a sound. A Calcutta newspaper published a story about these desperate children. Right away, Mother Teresa called, asking what she could do for the family. The newspaper had collected 7,000 rupees ($700.00) for the children. Mother put 5,000 rupees in the bank to be Rita's dowry and used the rest to help the children. The Missionaries of Charity Sisters raised them.

It was very difficult for many Indian children to go to school. They had only rags to wear and never enough food. They had no pencils or paper and there was almost no light to study by. Mother was determined that every child in her care who was able to learn would be given an education or special training to help them earn a living when they grew up. A wealthy Hindu lady from Calcutta paid the tuition for Mother Teresa's first ten children so that they could get a good education.

In spite of the sadness the children had known, Shishu Bhavan was full of laughter. The Sisters enjoyed working there. They carried the children in their arms, gave them piggy-back rides and swung them in the air. The eager smiling faces invited love and attention. "Look at them," Mother said. "They are hungry for love."

Shishu Bhavan became the center for work in Calcutta. Next to the main building there was a busy nurses' office and a huge kitchen where the Sisters were constantly cooking. From this kitchen, they fed 7,000 people every day and any day the Sisters did not cook, these people had no food to eat.

One afternoon, a Sister told Mother Teresa, "We've run out of bread, Mother. We will have to tell the people we have nothing to feed them today and tomorrow." Mother could not say anything. She put the matter in God's hands. Within a short time a truck drove up, followed by another. Both trucks were loaded with bread. For some unknown reason, the government had shut down all the schools for one day and decided to let Mother Teresa's poor have the bread the schoolchildren usually ate. There was so much bread. "God was thinking of us," Mother told the children. "He is taking such good care of us!"

The Sisters took care of unwed mothers, giving them a place to stay at Shishu Bhavan until their babies were born. If the mothers were unable to care for their babies, the Sisters would find a good home for them.

"One reason the world has so many problems," Mother said, "is people do not love each other enough. As soon as we all learn to love babies even before they are born, the world will be a better place for all of us."

One morning, a worried man came looking for Mother Teresa. "Mother, come quick!" he cried. "Please help me! My wife is about to kill our baby!" As soon as Mother heard the man, she hurried to him. They rushed to the hospital together. The man told her, "You see, Mother, we are very poor and we have a hard time feeding all of our daughters. So when my wife learned she was pregnant she took our last money and went to the doctor. She wants to kill our baby even before it is born because she doesn't know how we will be able to take care of it."

When they got to the hospital, the wife was already on the operating table. If they had arrived a few minutes later, it would have been too late. Mother Teresa talked to the woman. "God has given you this very precious gift. It is God's life that is in the unborn baby. Please don't let your baby die. God takes care of the flowers and the birds. He takes care of everything in the world that He has created. And these little children are His life. There can never be enough."

The woman listened to Mother Teresa and she began to cry. "I didn't want to hurt my baby, Mother," she said. "But I was so worried. I already have four daughters and it is so hard to take care of them. I didn't know what to do."

"The Sisters and I will help you and be with you when you need us," Mother promised her. The woman climbed down from the operating table and the three of them left the hospital together. Five months later, the woman gave birth to her first son and the whole family rejoiced.

Mother Teresa began a program for poor people who wanted to limit the number of children they had. "We are teaching our beggars, our leprosy patients, our street people how to be better parents, how to love one another and how to use self-control and natural family planning," Mother once told an audience in Calcutta.

"Isn't it strange for nuns to be teaching birth control?" a young woman asked.

Mother laughed. "Who is better able to teach a method of self-control than we who have taken vows of chastity?"

Mother was once given ninety-five cartons of powdered milk to feed the poor. These were put out in the courtyard of the Shishu Bhavan and soon it began to rain. The rain poured down without stopping for five days. "What are You doing, Lord?" cried Mother Teresa. "The milk is outside!" The worried Sisters prayed that the milk would not be ruined. When the rain finally stopped, they rushed out to inspect the damage. The boxes were floating in water, but the milk was perfectly dry. One box had a broken lid. When she started opening it, Mother Teresa asked, "God, what happened to this one?" But not one drop of water had entered the broken box. "What earthly spouse would have taken such good care of his family?" Mother asked. "God is so good to us."

Mother Teresa once found a child of six or seven on the streets. "I took her to Shishu Bhavan and gave her a bath, some clothes and nice food. That evening she ran away. We found her a second time and a third time and she kept running away. After the third time, I sent a Sister to follow her. The Sister found the child sitting with her mother and sister under a tree. There was a little dish there and the mother was sharing food she had picked up on the streets. They were eating right there on the street. They were sleeping right there. It was their home. And we understood why the child ran away. The mother loved the child and the child loved the mother. They were so good to each other. The child was happy. She was at home. Her mother was her home."

There was another child who came to the children's home around midnight one night. Mother Teresa saw her standing just outside the gate. She went down and found her in tears. "What's wrong?" she asked.

"My mother doesn't want me," the little girl sobbed. "My father doesn't want me. Nobody wants me."

"I want you!" Mother Teresa told her, and she took the child to Shishu Bhavan, where there was always room enough for one more child.

Shanti Nagar

One day in 1957, five lepers came to Mother Teresa for help. "Our families are afraid they will catch our sickness so they sent us away. We have all lost our jobs and have no place to live and nothing to eat." They had been searching for food in garbage cans. Mother helped set up a shelter for them in a house at Gobra on the outskirts of Calcutta. She and her Sisters washed their sores, gave them medicine, milk and rice, doing everything they could to help the lepers feel loved and cared for. More lepers came to live there and soon they had a sanctuary for over 150 patients.

Within eight months the government decided to use this land for something else. They told Mother Teresa they were going to tear down the house where the lepers lived and build houses for other poor people. Mother Teresa was determined to save the lepers' home. She went to see a good friend of hers, Dr. B.C. Roy, the Chief Minister of Bengal. Dr. Roy was a medical doctor who had taken care of many famous people in India. He had been the family doctor for Mahatma Gandhi, the King of Nepal, and Prime Minister Nehru. Dr. Roy was busy with government affairs, but he gave one hour of free medical care to poor people each morning in his own home.

Mother Teresa had met him not long after she had begun her work in Calcutta. She had gone to his house early one morning. His secretary opened the door and invited Mother to sit down on one of the wooden benches in the doctor's hallway. Dr. Roy came in and looked at each patient's face, examined his or her eyes and tongue. He spent a few minutes with each, decided what was wrong, told them what medicine they needed and what to do, then he went on to the next patient. No time was wasted. When the doctor came to Mother Teresa, she said, "I didn't come to you for my health. Can you help us get water for the people who live in the huts at Motijihl?"

Dr. Roy immediately wrote a letter asking the Calcutta Water Department to handle this matter for Mother Teresa. Mother kept coming back to the doctor asking for more help for the poor people.

The next time she went to see Dr. Roy, he said, "Mother Teresa, you can call on me at my office any time. You don't need an appointment." He was a man who cared about people and was trying to help his country. He and Mother Teresa trusted each other and worked together helping the poorest of the poor.

But now, Mother Teresa had to ask for help for the lepers at Gobra. "Please, Dr. Roy," she pleaded, "You have to help them save their home. They have no place else to go."

Dr. Roy shook his head sadly. "They will have to find another place, Mother. Calcutta has to grow. The city is overcrowded, and we have to find homes for all the homeless people. We can't let 150 lepers get in the way of all the other poor people."

"But what about the lepers?" Mother asked. "They have lost their families, their jobs, everything they have ever had. They are not welcome anywhere. Where will they go? Promise me you won't make them leave until we've found them a place."

"What about the Bankura district?" Dr. Roy suggested.

"The Bankura district?" Mother gasped. "The Bankura district doesn't even have water. Leprosy patients have to have enough water."

"We'll find them a place," Dr. Roy promised.

Although Mother Teresa was not able to prevent the government from transferring the lepers from Gobra to another location, she was able to delay the move until adequate installations were made available.

To draw attention to the problems facing the lepers, Mother Teresa's helpers and the Missionaries of Charity started a Flag Day Leprosy Fund. They organized street collections all over Calcutta with cans that read: "Touch a leper with your compassion." Various social organizations joined in collecting money using that same motto. It was an appeal for love and mercy as well as money. The whole city became aware of the sad plight of the lepers and moved to do something about it.

When someone told Mother Teresa, "I wouldn't touch a leper for a million dollars," she replied, "Neither would I. But I would gladly do so for the love of God."

On his eightieth birthday, Dr. Roy went to his office as usual. Reporters asked him, "Dr. Roy, how do you feel still being Chief Minister at the age of eighty?"

He said simply, "As I climbed the steps leading to my office this morning, I thought of Mother Teresa who devotes her life to the welfare of the poor." The next day, it was front page news in Calcutta. Mother Teresa, who saw Christ in the poorest of the poor and strove to be one of them, had become a superstar in Calcutta.

This publicity brought more women asking to join her order, more helpers, money and supplies. Mother Teresa had always hated being in the public eye because she was convinced it was God's work she was doing, and all the glory should go to Him. It always made her sad to hear herself praised.

Mother Teresa learned that new drugs like Dapsone and Sulfone relieved the suffering in the most advanced stages and that leprosy could be arrested if discovered in time. Up until that time, leprosy had been treated only in special hospitals called leprosariums. But there were only a few of these and each one could handle only a few hundred people. Lepers were reluctant to go to the leprosariums because everyone would know they had the disease. Once it became known a person had contracted leprosy, he or she became a complete outcast. They would lose their homes, their jobs, their families. People were afraid even to come near them. The discovery of the new drugs allowed patients to be treated outside the hospital. Now they could live at home and still receive regular treatments.

Once, a businessman told his wife, "I have discovered the early signs."

"We have two daughters," his wife said. "If it's known you are a leper, they will never get husbands. You must leave home."

He left the house and was planning to commit suicide until the Sisters discovered him in the bustees. They convinced him to try the new drugs; his disease was cured and he became one of Mother's helpers.

Mother learned that leprosy was not nearly as contagious as most people thought. "There are risks of infection involved in touching them," Mother told her Sisters, "but these are risks that we are prepared to take in order to help our dear lepers." All of the Sisters agreed they would be willing to tend the wounds of the lepers but some were afraid. "How will we know if we have caught the disease?" one young Sister asked.

"Speak with the doctors," Mother told them, "and do whatever they tell you to do."

The doctors said, "Do not touch any of the patients who are actively contagious."

"What should I do?" asked a Sister tending to a very old woman who appeared to be contagious.

"Obey the doctor, Sister," Mother told her as she helped the old woman up the steps. "Do not run the danger. Do all the things the doctors told you to do. Then you will be better able to help the patients and for a longer time."

Originally, Mother had planned to set up leprosy clinics in seven districts where she knew there were lepers. One was in Motijihl, but a well-known businessman complained, "We can't have a clinic here. It's too close to home." Mother tried to convince him how essential it was that India's lepers be cared for, but he insisted, "I don't care what you do for them just as long as you don't do it in my back yard." The man turned some important congressmen against the leper clinics, so Mother got the idea for mobile clinics. "We shall go out to leper colonies with ambulances, giving advice, medicine and Christian love to these, the most unwanted of all people, Christ in His most distressing disguise." She went to the businessman who had fought against the clinics. "Bless you, Sir," she said. "I just want to thank you. You have made our job much easier by inspiring us to use mobile clinics."

During the next two months, a large electric company donated 10,000 rupees. A Hindu specialist in leprosy, Dr. Sen, retired from his job at the Hospital for Tropical Diseases and offered his services exclusively to Mother.

Mother Teresa had been given a van in 1956 by Catholic Relief Services for her Mother and Child Mobile Clinics throughout Calcutta. On September 1, 1957, Archbishop Perier officially opened Mother's first mobile clinic for Leprosy. The celebration took place at Shishu Bhavan, the Calcutta children's home. The mobile van visited four bustees each week: Motijihl, Howrah, Dappa and Tiljala.

Even with the mobile clinics, there was still a need for hospitals and villages for lepers in the last stages of their disease, those who were contagious or unable to care for themselves. Mother Teresa was determined to build the small villages where they could live, work, and raise their children.

The town of Barrackpore was a small village with paper mills, jute mills and rows of shanties on stilts over drains where 250 homeless lepers lived. The local Methodist minister had a little land he wanted to develop for the lepers. He asked the Anglican bishop for financial assistance. Together they explained the situation to Mother Teresa, who was eager to get the lepers settled. The city gave her more land.

In March 1959, the first permanent leprosy clinic was opened. The name was changed to Titagarh. Only those who were contagious or in the last stages could live there.

Ann Blaikie represented Mother at the opening. At the clinic the lepers received the medicines they needed and were trained in self-help. They learned to weave their own bandages, make shoes out of foam rubber and old tires, sew their own clothing and to do simple carpentry. They even built their own houses.

One of the biggest problems facing the Sisters was the lack of money for the medicine. There were leper parents whose small children had not yet caught the disease, but who would become lepers if they did not receive the necessary drugs in time.

"Separate all the children from their parents," some people suggested.

But Mother refused. "How can human beings, deprived of everything by their disease, be without the warmth of their children, and how can innocent children be snatched from their tender, loving parents?"

While looking for another site for a leper clinic, Mother found a plot of land between two railway lines. She and Ann Blaikie went to examine the land. An angry crowd of villagers was waiting for them. When they arrived, a village official asked the crowd, "Do you want a leper clinic here?" The people shouted, "No! Go away! Leave us alone!" They began to pick up stones and sticks and hurled them at Mother Teresa and her helper. The two women ran back to their car ducking the stones.

"I don't think God wants us to have a leper clinic here," Mother sighed. "Oh, well, we'll pray for two months and then we'll see where He does want the clinic."

In Calcutta, there was not one hospital that specialized in leprosy even though over 40,000 lepers lived in the city.

It was Mother Teresa's dream to build a real home for lepers. Shanti Nagar, the City of Peace, answered that prayer. It was built at Asansol, the village where Mother Teresa had lived while waiting for Papal permission to leave the Loreto Sisters and go into the streets. The Indian government donated 34 acres of land and the Sisters and lepers planted trees, cared for flower gardens, and stocked ponds with fish. Volunteers taught the lepers how to make bricks and build their own cottages.

There were comfortable wards for the seriously ill and small cottages where families could live together. When their disease was arrested, parents lived with their children. But there was also a nursery for children born at Shanti Nager to parents who were contagious. The lepers planted their own rice and wheat, raised their own cattle and kept their own chickens. They wove baskets to sell and even started their own printing press. There were community kitchens, workshops and a school for the children. Since the lepers were taught many new skills, they were no longer forced to beg for a living. Their greatest joy came from knowing they were no longer hated or feared, but loved and cared for by Mother and her Sisters. They had their own home where they could live and die with dignity, do meaningful work and lead lives as close to normal as possible.

Mother put Sister Francis Xavier Orzes, a medical doctor, in charge of the City of Peace. Sister Francis Xavier was a few years younger than Mother Teresa, born in Yugoslavia, and had been a Sister of Loreto like Mother before joining the Missionaries of Charity. Sister Francis Xavier was a cheerful, talkative, energetic nun who kept Shanti Nagar well scrubbed, comfortable and pleasant. Her skills at interior decorating, placing a touch of color here and a vase of flowers there, made her a true blessing to the City of Peace. The fact that she had taken a vow to serve the poorest of the poor was God's gift to the lepers of Asansol. She was a real builder and doer, and her mind was always filled with plans to improve the gardens, enhance the wards, or buy a printing press for the lepers. She sent hope flowing through the community.

Some of the lepers had trouble with the police. Sajada, a middle-aged man, had been in prison for murder. He would hang around Shanti Nagar for a while and then disappear for several months. The Sisters would beg him, "Please come for your medicine so you won't have to suffer so much." When the pain got too bad, he would come again for a few days of treatment. Then when he felt better again, he would go off to drink. One day he was in such pain that he took a knife and cut off one of his sores and almost bled to death. When he drank he became angry, cursed loudly, started fights and often found himself in jail. He had been coming to the clinic for many years and the Sisters loved him even though he hardly ever smiled or showed them any affection. He said, "You Sisters surprise me. You have proven to me you love everyone, even bad people like me."

One day when Mother Teresa came to visit Shanti Nagar, Sister Francis Xavier asked her, "May I speak with you alone, Mother?"

"Of course, Sister."

They went to the sacristy of the little chapel.

"I have leprosy, Mother," Sister Francis said calmly. "There are several Sisters who have been diagnosed."

"Let's pray and turn the situation over to the Master of the house," Mother said.

They spent some time in prayer. Then Sister Francis said, "I'm sorry, Mother. I'm sorry we did not follow Doctor Sen's rules not to touch those with contagious wounds. But when you see Jesus in His distressing disguise and you know He gladly died for you, how can you put worries about your own health before caring for Him?"

"I know, Sister," Mother Teresa said. "I never told any of you not to touch them. I told all of you to listen to the doctors very carefully so you will understand the situation. Would you like to come to the Mother House in Calcutta until you are healed?"

"No, thank you, Mother Teresa. We have discussed this and all of us have decided to remain here with our lepers." They refused any special care or hospital, choosing to remain among the lepers.

All the Sisters were cured as the disease was caught early and treated with the new and powerful drugs. Sister Francis remained in charge of Shanti Nagar.

Rome Via Las Vegas

Mother Teresa left India for the first time in thirty-one years to go to Las Vegas, Nevada. She was invited to speak to the National Council of Catholic Women at their annual meeting. The year was 1960. When she received the invitation, Mother asked aloud, "I wonder why they want me?"

"Who wants you, Mother?" Sister Frederick asked.

"The National Council of Catholic Women . . . all the way over in America. Surely they could find a speaker a little closer to them."

"Everyone wants to hear you talk about Jesus and His work, Mother," Sister Frederick assured her.

Mother called Archbishop Perier for his advice. "I'm delighted that those Catholic women in America have invited you," the Archbishop said. "Yes, Mother, you should definitely go."

"The idea of speaking to a large crowd terrifies me," Mother told him.

"Just trust the Holy Spirit to handle your speech for you."

"Oh, Your Grace, the Holy Spirit handles everything I do. But I still find myself nervous before and after I speak, even to the smallest audience."

On a brisk October day, Mother Teresa flew into Las Vegas without any of her Sisters. She was met by Eileen Egan, head of American Catholic Relief Services.

"How was your trip, Mother?" Eileen asked cheerfully.

"It was fine," Mother said. "But tell me why everyone around me laughed when I asked for a ticket to Las Vegas."

Eileen laughed. "Well, Mother. Las Vegas is known for its gambling, drinking and quick marriages after Reno divorces. There aren't too many nuns who travel great distances to come here."

"It sounds like a good place to have a meeting of Catholic women," Mother said without a smile, her eyes dancing.

"Actually, Mother, we didn't choose Las Vegas. It chose us. The city officials offered us a free convention hall for our meetings and exhibits, and we couldn't get a better offer anywhere."

Just then, Cardinal Cushing, Archbishop of Boston, noticed Mother Teresa and came over to say hello. "Mahatma Gandhi," he said smiling broadly. "I am so happy to meet you."

"I am happy to meet you too, Your Grace. And I'm pleased if you think of Mahatma Gandhi when you see me."

Pope John XXIII had sent his blessing. He wrote to the women, "You have the consolation of knowing that these works of love performed on behalf of those united to you only by the bond of charity will last beyond the other good works of your lifetime. They will go with you into eternity and help you to unite with the source of all love, God."

Eileen Egan could not understand why Mother Teresa was so nervous about speaking at the convention. "You've spoken to many groups before, Mother," Eileen said, hoping to relax her.

"I've never spoken outside of Calcutta before," Mother said.

To help Mother prepare herself for her talk, Eileen Egan drove her to the Nevada desert. Mother settled herself next to a cactus plant praying silently in the hot sun. Then she bent over and collected a few long cactus spines which she twisted into a crown of thorns.

Later that day, inside a large banquet room, over 3,000 women examined Mother Teresa's cheap white cotton sari and her bare feet in simple sandals. They had never seen a Catholic nun dressed in such a way. Mother sat saying her Rosary as a well-dressed woman elaborately described her work in Calcutta and then introduced her. Mother walked to the front of the crowd, placed her hands together palm to palm, and bowed her head. "This is the way we greet people in India," Mother began, her eyes caressing the crowd. She continued, "I have never spoken in public before. This is the first time, and to be here with you and be able to tell you the love story of God's mercy for the poorest of the poor, it is the grace of God."

When Mother Teresa began speaking of her people and the work, she forgot her fears, relaxed, and spoke enthusiastically of God's love in action. She told of a Muslim woman suffering the last stages of tuberculosis who brought her son to Mother. Mother said that the woman told her, "'My days are counted. Give him a home. Love him.' I told her, 'Well, as long as you are alive, come twice or three times a day to see the child.' And this very sick woman walked four miles every day to see her child. She loved the child in a heroic way. She would not touch him and begged me, 'Mother, take my child in your arms. When I see you loving him, I will be happy. I can't touch my son because if I touch him, I may give him my disease.'"

The women in the audience could visualize the poor in India, just as Mother herself did when she was a little girl listening to the missionary telling his tale.

"I am not going to ask you for further aid. We depend completely on the loving Providence of God. People only need to know the needs of their fellow human beings. I don't beg. I have not begged from the time we started this work. We merely go to Hindus, Muslims, and Christians and tell them, "I have come to give you a chance to do something beautiful for God."

The women stood and applauded.

"So again I thank you for all you have done and may God continue to bless you one and all." She put her hands together once more and bowed to them, then quietly returned to her seat.

During the four days of the convention, Mother Teresa spent much of her time in the exhibit hall in a booth entitled "The Works of Peace" with photos of American Catholic women working with the needy overseas. Many people asked her, "Mother, why do you wear the white sari with the blue trim?"

"This inexpensive cotton sari is what the poor women of India wear. We chose the blue trim because Our Lady is often shown wearing blue and it reminds us that the Blessed Mother is the cause of our joy. She brought Jesus into the world for us, and is eager to bring each of us to Him."

They had many questions for her:

"What country were you born in, Mother Teresa?"

"Doesn't it frighten you to work with lepers?"

"What is your home for the dying really like?"

Mother Teresa always carried with her a big bag made from a piece of army cloth with a wooden handle. Without a word, the women put money into her bag. The women were as moved by her presence as they were by her message. She glowed with the love of the Lord. She had a smile for each woman who approached her, and she made each one feel loved and cherished.

While the convention was going on, the entertainment and gambling activity continued night and day. On her way from the convent where she was staying, Mother looked at the electric signs, the nightclubs, the flashing lights.

"What do you think of Las Vegas, Mother?" asked one of the women.

"It reminds me of the Hindu Festival of Lights," she said.

Every time Cardinal Cushing passed her, he would say, "Hello, Mahatma Gandhi. So wonderful to have you with us."

"Thank you, Your Grace," she would say with a big smile.

Mother asked Eileen Egan to accompany her to Rome on the way back to Calcutta. Eileen agreed. Mother had finished a Constitution which, if approved, would recognize the Missionaries of Charity as a Society of Pontifical Right. This meant that Mother Teresa's order would be under the protection of Rome, not just the Archbishop of Calcutta, and would then be able go outside India to carry out their work. The Constitution had been approved by many priests who were friends of Mother's, and now she was taking it to the Pope for his approval.

She wrote to her Sisters: "I shall begin a novena to the Sacred Heart November 11th. I am going to try to see our Holy Father and beg him to take our little society under his special care with a Pontifical recognition. We are not worthy of this great gift, but if it is God's will, we will get it. Pray and make sacrifices." Mother wanted to be able to open houses any place in the world.

Rome, the Eternal City, where the Vatican is located, has been a place of pilgrimage for Catholics for many centuries. It is where the Pope lives, where St. Peter was crucified. Many great saints such as St. Agnes, St. Sebastian and St. Cecilia had hidden and were buried in the catacombs. Mother Teresa had never been there and was thrilled at the chance to go.

As soon as she was safely fastened in her seat, Mother took out her beads and began saying the Rosary. "Lord, if You want us to become a world-wide organization where we can serve the poorest of Your poor wherever they most need Your tender care, You know what You must do." Mother said three Rosaries, read a few chapters of her prayer book and fell soundly asleep.

When the plane landed in Rome, Mother tried to control her excitement. Besides seeing the Eternal City for the first time, she was going to see her beloved brother Lazar after thirty years.

Mother was staying in a Roman convent where she could not have any guests. The Christian Brothers of Ireland let her use their school parlor so she could meet with her brother, his wife and daughter. Lazar was now fifty-three years old. He had been living in Palermo, Italy for many years. When Mother entered, Lazar stood, rushed toward her and threw his arms around her.

"Gonxha!" he said. "I've missed you."

"Lazar! I've missed you."

"I guess I was wrong when I said you were burying yourself," he said with a laugh. "You certainly don't look buried."

"So this is your wife?" Mother asked.

"Yes," Lazar said proudly. "This is Maria. She is the heroine who threw herself on top of me when some Albanian partisans were trying to kill me."

Mother Teresa squeezed Maria's hand. "Thank you for loving my Lazar so much. Thank you for saving his life."

Maria gave her a slight, embarrassed smile. "The would-be killers changed their minds, thank God," she said.

"I remember you wrote about that during the last days of the war," Mother said to Lazar.

Turning back to her sister-in-law, Mother said, "Maria, I am so happy to meet you at last."

They hugged. "Me too," Maria said.

"And this is our daughter, Agi. She's ten years old."

Mother leaned toward the beautiful little girl with her arms outstretched. Agi hugged her new-found aunt.

"It's so wonderful to be together again," Lazar said. "If only our mother and Aga could be here."

"It was beautiful when we were able to get letters back and forth to Albania on a regular basis," Mother said. "It's been such a long time since we had any news from them."

In 1932, Lazar had arranged for his sister Aga to join him in Tirana, Albania. Aga, who had a degree in economics, found work as a translator and eventually worked as a broadcaster for Radio Tirana. In 1934, Lazar and Aga had convinced their mother to sell her home in Skopje and live with them in Albania. The three of them lived together until Lazar went away to fight in the Second World War. Many men had found Aga attractive and several had asked for her hand in marriage. But she loved her mother, and felt it her duty to care for her as long as she lived.

Both Mother Teresa and Lazar had kept in touch with Drana and Aga until the Marxist regime had closed the iron curtain and cut off all communication with the outside world. Drana and Aga felt very isolated, longing to see Mother Teresa and Lazar.

"I contacted everyone I could think of," Lazar said, "trying to find some way to bring them to Italy. My friends in the French diplomatic corps were the only ones who even received a reply. Finally, I was able to get a letter from Aga. They were lonely and sad, but they were healthy. I haven't given up. We will keep praying and I will keep working with my friends from the Embassy."

"Yes," Mother Teresa said. "God willing, we will all be together one day soon."

Mother Teresa was invited to a Mass celebrated by Pope John XXIII in the Sistine Chapel under Michelangelo's frescoes of Creation and The Last Judgment. She was so excited she said, "Now I can carry each one of my Missionaries to the feet of Christ's Vicar on earth. I will carry them just as they are, and I am sure with his fatherly love, he will bless each one, and obtain for them the graces they need to become saints."

As the Pope was leaving the chapel, Mother stepped forward to kiss his ring. No one else did. He paused in the procession to give her his blessing.

The morning Mother Teresa was to take her Constitution to the Vatican, she knocked on the door of Eileen Egan's room. "Could you please type this for me?" she asked, showing Eileen her two single spaced pages containing a broad outline of the unique mission of the Missionaries of Charity. Her friend, who was not a proficient typist, became nervous at the idea of typing the pages such a short time before the appointment, but she managed to finish it on time with no errors just as Mother Teresa had assured her she would.

Carrying the papers, Mother went to the Sacred Congregation for the Propagation of the Faith. Eileen Egan accompanied her. As they walked through the many corridors, they heard the words "Madre Fondatrice" (Founding Mother) repeated by passersby. Finally they arrived in the presence of Gregory Cardinal Agagianian and Archbishop Pietro Sigismondi.

"Please sit down," the Cardinal said, motioning toward two plush red velvet chairs. Mother continued saying her Rosary while the two churchmen bent over the freshly typed papers she had given them. They discussed her notes in Italian.

Cardinal Agagianian asked Mother Teresa many questions. "What kind of work do the Sisters do? What training have they had? What is this fourth vow of wholehearted and free service to the poorest of the poor?" The Cardinal said, "I don't understand how you expect to exist and work in a mission land without a regular source of income."

"We put our trust completely in the Lord," Mother told him. "He has not ever deserted us. He has seen us through so far. Of course, our Sisters have few material needs since we live a life of poverty in dress and housing. We don't want to have more than the poor who live around us."

The Cardinal and the Archbishop examined the Sisters' prayer book. It was printed in English on very inexpensive paper. The Archbishop said, "This book has no formal permission."

"They are poor," the Cardinal explained.

They thanked Mother Teresa for coming and told her, "You will be hearing from us, Mother."

Now that her mission was completed, Mother Teresa was eager to return to her Sisters at the Mother House in Calcutta. Her brother Lazar saw her off at the Rome airport. "I will continue to do everything I can to get Mother and Aga out of Albania," he promised.

"I know you will," she said. "My prayers will be with you. Take good care of your family," Mother told her brother.

"And you take good care of yours," Lazar said.

Branching Out

During the autumn of 1962, Pope John XXIII summoned all bishops worldwide to Rome for a Vatican Council. Two council fathers struck up a conversation that was to play an important part in bringing the Missionaries of Charity to the New World. At a coffee bar underneath St. Peter's church, Bishop Benitez of Venezuela talked with the Papal Internuncio to New Delhi, Archbishop James Robert Knox, about the lack of priests and religious in South America. They were so engrossed in the conversation they continued it for days.

"There are many areas in my Diocese where the poor receive no medical care at all," Bishop Benitez said. "There is a special section where Afro-Venezuelans live in great poverty. They were brought in to work the copper mines and never given any education. They work for almost nothing. I'm afraid that these poor people are being exploited. They are being terribly mistreated and neglected. We need religious Sisters to live and work with our women."

Archbishop Knox described the Missionaries of Charity to Archbishop Benitez, who became very excited. "Yes, that is exactly what my Diocese needs!"

Archbishop Knox said, "I will tell Mother Teresa about your Diocese."

Archbishop Benitez said, "Be sure to give her my invitation to set up a house there."

Archbishop Knox reminded him, "Of course, they can't leave India until their order is approved by the Pope. But that should not be too long in coming."

In the fall of 1964, Mother Teresa accepted Bishop Benitez's invitation to visit Venezuela and took Eileen Egan with her. At Barquisimito airport, the vicar in charge of religious for the Diocese welcomed them to Venezuela. "The Bishop has arranged for you to be the guest of the Salesian Sisters at their boarding school."

Everywhere Mother looked she saw lovely jacarandas in bloom. She took a short nap each afternoon, something she had never done before. Someone asked her about it, and she said, "Oh, it's the medication I'm taking because of the road mishap at Darjeeling." Earlier that year, Mother had been in a jeep with Bishop Eric Benjamin traveling on an old military road. Coming around a bend, they met a truck head-on. Mother Teresa fell forward, striking her head, and was badly cut. Mother had insisted it was nothing, but she was taken to Planter's Hospital in Darjeeling where she received nineteen stitches. The doctors told her if the wound had been a little lower, she would have lost an eye. The doctors also examined Mother Teresa and they were alarmed to note that her heart was being overworked. The doctors emphatically advised her to take it easy and gave her a medication to ensure that she would. She took it for awhile and then decided, "I must stop taking this. There's too much to do to waste my afternoons sleeping."

Two Spanish priests, Father Tomas and Father Manuel, showed Mother Teresa and Eileen Egan around Venezuela. "There is a real lack of priests and religious here. There are three priests who serve 35 communities," they explained. The priests took them to the jungle where the Afro-Venezuelans lived in houses built of mud and bamboo.

"Spanish priests come to Venezuela for five years at a time. Of course, some of them spend the rest of their lives here. These houses are replicas of dwellings in African villages," the priests said. "A few houses are made of brick and some of cement painted blue, but as you can see most of them are very crude." Half-naked children came out of the huts and stared at Mother and her companions. "This is Mother Teresa," Father Tomas told the children. "She wants to come back with some Sisters to help you."

The two priests took Mother and Eileen to the little chapel in the Black Zone. They opened up the church and rang the bells in celebration of their special guests.

Father gave a brief talk telling them how much he loved the time he had spent with them. Then he said, "I have brought you someone who wants to meet you and work with you and let you know how much God loves you. Mother Teresa has come all the way from India to be with you." Mother stood up, put her palms together, bowed to them and said, "God bless each and every one."

When they arrived at the village of Cocorote, they went straight to the small Spanish colonial church dedicated to St. Jeronimo. "One of us says Mass regularly in Cocorote," Father Tomas said. "Then our Sisters will come here," Mother replied. "I will put their spiritual care in your hands, Father Tomas and Father Manuel."

On May 2, 1965, the Pope recognized the Missionaries of Charity as a Society of Pontifical Right, giving them permission to work outside of India. Mother Teresa had long awaited this blessing which allowed her Sisters to serve the poor wherever in the world they were needed.

When the Sisters went to the Indian government offices to apply for passports and visas for Venezuela, there was much excitement.

"This is a change," a government worker said. "We have always been the country that received missionaries."

"Yes," Mother said, "but India is now the country that sends the missionaries."

"We have one problem though," the man said. "No rupees can be brought out of the country."

"That's all right," Mother said. "On my return from Venezuela, I spoke at a meeting of the Diocesan Council of Catholic Women and they have promised to sponsor us."

Within a year after her initial visit to Venezuela, Mother sent a team of four Sisters to make their headquarters in Cocorote. Within months she sent three more Sisters. The original group was all Indian: Sister Nirmala, Sister Pauline, Sister Justin, Sister Rosario, Sister Paul, and Sister Dolores.

The Bishop and the local people had prepared a luxurious home for the Sisters, but Mother had them give everything away. The poor people made a huge line around the convent when the word went out that the Sisters were giving away their luxuries. The neighbors made dresses and bedspreads out of the drapes. The family that received the refrigerator did not have electricity so they put the beautiful new appliance on its back, filled it with ice from the refrigerator of a little wealthier friend who had electricity and they had an old-fashioned ice box.

The rectory of the little church became their convent. There was a bare wooden table and several simple chairs. Someone donated a station wagon and taught the Sisters how to drive. They painted it a bright blue and drove to all the isolated villages.

The Sisters taught sewing, typing and English. They became a bridge between the people who had all they needed and those who had nothing. A butcher donated meat and stewing chickens. A poor man with a small business selling tortillas donated a few every day. The Sisters helped the priests prepare the children for their first Communion. The children called the Sisters "our sisters" because their skin was dark, the same shade as the children's.

Someone offered the Sisters a site for a community center. It was a city block containing the ruins of a hotel that had been abandoned long ago. It had become the town garbage dump with weeds and bushes all about.

When Mother Teresa and the Sisters arrived, some men came running. "Don't walk in the grass!" they warned. "There are many snakes!" The Sisters looked worried, but Mother smiled and said, "The space is good. Let's get the people to help us clean it up and see what we can do with it." The local people cleared out the dump and the Sisters used the location for training and for a refuge for the homeless and abandoned.

"Our Sisters do almost everything," Mother said. "They preach. They lead the prayers. They even give out Holy Communion. The only thing they can't do is celebrate the Mass."

"What about confessions?" someone asked. "They can't hear confessions."

"They hear confessions all the time," Mother said. "They just can't give absolution."

Sister Leonia, a medical doctor who was in charge of the house in Raigarh, India, came to Venezuela for a meeting of the Sisters. She was brushing her teeth when she began coughing. She had spasms and made dry gagging sounds. The Sisters rushed her to the hospital. The doctors took one look at her and said, "This looks serious. We have to do some tests immediately." One of the doctors returned, looking very serious. "I'm sorry," he said, "but she has rabies." Sister Leonia had her eyes shut and he thought she was unconscious.

"What can we do?" a Sister asked him.

"Pray," the doctor said, "That's all any of us can do. She will be dead within 48 hours."

Several Sisters remembered that months earlier, back in Raigarh, Sister Leonia had rescued a puppy from a pack of wild dogs and one of the dogs had bitten her. She had cauterized the wound but rabies was very difficult to prevent.

Sister Leonia overheard the doctor saying she would be dead in 48 hours. "Oh, no!" she cried. "There is so much work to do. I can't die now!"

Mother Teresa and the other Sisters brought her back to the house. Mother sat by her, took her hand and said, "I have received you into this work for Jesus. I will be with you to help you get ready to go from us to Him."

Sister Leonia relaxed, but then her body was overcome by terrible spasms. The Sisters called the doctor, who came right away. The spasms continued but Sister Leonia was preparing herself to go home to her Lord and all of her attention was on Him.

"I've never seen anyone with such superhuman control," the doctor said. "She has been so silent. Most people with rabies scream and shout. It is a horrible pain."

Mother Teresa was by her side when Sister Leonia died 45 hours later.

While Mother was in Venezuela, the Sisters told her, "There's a desperate need for a house for unwed mothers. We have so many young girls who have no place to wait for their babies."

The governor of the state of Vargas was also aware of this need and eager to do something. "Mother Teresa," he said, "Please look for a suitable location. If you find the right place our civil authorities will take care of the finances." When the Sisters found a site, the lawyer who represented the landowners suggested a meeting for all the people involved in the decision. The governor told Mother Teresa, "I am unable to attend this meeting, but if you reach an agreement with the owners, we will pay whatever price you agree upon." The lawyer said, "The owner is asking

5,000,000 bolivars" (approximately one million dollars). Mother could not believe what she was hearing. She raised her arms in the air and a loud "No!" issued from her lips. Then she said loudly, "You do not speculate with the poor!" She absolutely refused to negotiate. The lawyer returned to the landowner with Mother's refusal.

A few days later, the governor called Mother and asked, "Did you reach an agreement on the house?"

"No, Sir," she said. "The owner is trying to take advantage of the poor."

"You didn't see any way to work something out?" he asked.

Mother said, "I can't even imagine what would happen if we accepted such abuse at the expense of the poor."

"No matter what else we lose," Mother told her Sisters, "we must always guard our poverty. If we are to understand and help those who have nothing, we must live like them and with them." In spite of this setback, Mother and her Sisters were able to establish a foothold in Venezuela which would eventually take root and grow.

Mother Teresa was often asked to start a religious order for men. By 1963, she saw a real need for them in her work. A few men wanted her to form a Congregation of Brothers similar to the Missionaries of Charity Sisters. They would be taught in the same spirit and work with the Sisters as needed.

In the beginning, Father Julien Henry, Mother's friend from her teaching days at St. Mary's, helped her teach her Brothers, but he did not feel called to be one of them. On March 25, 1963, Archbishop Albert D'Souza blessed the new branch and they began their work though Rome had not yet agreed to have the Missionaries of Charity Brothers as part of the official church.

In 1964, Father Ian Traves-Bell, an Australian Jesuit priest, came to spend a few weeks at Shishu Bhavan (the children's home in Calcutta). He was a tall, thin young man with a warm personality and a quick smile. He had a neat beard and twinkling eyes. "I'm here to check up on you," he said.

Father Traves-Bell was amazed by the Missionaries' love for people, their dedication and devotion. He saw Mother Teresa working hard all day and writing letters half the night. He watched the new Brothers, so intense in their prayer and in their work.

The day before he left to return to his Jesuit order, he and Mother Teresa walked in the playground with the children calling Mother and tugging at her sari.

"Father, have you thought about giving yourself to the poorest of the poor?" Mother asked him.

"I love working with the poor," he told her, "but I could never give myself to them completely the way you do, Mother."

She told him, "None of us can give ourselves completely to anything unless the Lord is calling us. Then it is not us. It is He who does the work."

Father Traves-Bell said, "I am too ordinary, too settled in my work." He wrote books explaining Christianity to non-Christian readers.

"Let's just put it all in God's hands," Mother said.

"Of course, Mother," he said. "We are all in His hands."

The next day he left Calcutta with no plans of returning. In less than a year, Father Traves-Bell was back in Calcutta.

Mother was surprised to see him. "Father, what brings you back to us?"

"You told me of your second call, Mother. Well, I too have received a call within a call. I feel called to work with you, Mother. I'm ready to give myself to Jesus in the poorest of the poor."

"Will you be my General Servant for the Missionaries of Charity Brothers?" Mother asked.

"As soon as I am released from the Jesuits," he promised.

The Jesuit priests were very helpful to Father Traves-Bell. They gave him permission to leave the Jesuits and encouraged him to become a Missionaries of Charity Brother. He became Brother Andrew, General Servant of the Missionaries of Charity Brothers.

"He is a very holy person," Mother said. "I am happy to put the Brothers in his charge." It was a great help to have a young priest who was full of energy, and who loved God and His poor. "What will the Brothers wear?" Mother asked Brother Andrew.

"We'll have no special clothes. We will wear simple pants and shirts with a crucifix on the shoulder."

Mother Teresa would have preferred for the Brothers to wear clothes that identified them as Missionaries of Charity but she was determined to let them make their own decisions.

Mother Teresa was delighted to have a General Servant and a real beginning for an official organization of Brothers. "There will be some priests as well as Brothers among you," she said, "so you can open houses from a church." There were fewer Brothers than Sisters, but their life was the same, working for the very poor and the very ill. Their way of life was difficult, but they were joyful because they knew they were doing God's will. They worked hard among the poorest people and they lived like the poor. They ate simple food, wore plain clothes, and shared whatever they had. They worked with lepers, young people with problems, sick people, homeless children, and the dying. They helped people to find work. They worked with boys in Mother Teresa's schools. They made homes for homeless children and helped alcoholics and drug addicts.

Brother Andrew adapted the Brothers' teachings and way of life to be like the poor people they were working with.

Many men wanted to join but were not emotionally or physically strong enough. The New Testament describes Jesus as saying "come and see" when asked where He lived. Brother Andrew invited young men to "come and see" what the life was like. He called those who accepted his invitation "come and sees." Mother Teresa took over the term also for young women who wanted to experience the Sister's life before making a commitment.

When Brother Andrew first joined the Missionaries of Charity Brothers, there were twelve young men eager to give their lives to working with the poor. They lived on the first floor of Shishu Bhavan. Right away, they began searching for a headquarters of their own and found a three story house at 7 Mansatala Row, Kidderpore, Calcutta. Their first works of love developed out of the Missionaries of Charity Sisters' works. The Brothers cared for the men in the Home for the Dying and for the male lepers.

One day the Sisters found a young crippled boy, who was mentally retarded, playing on the streets. "What's your name?" they asked.

"My name is Johnny Walker," he said proudly.

"Where do you live?" they asked.

"Wherever I am," he said.

"Do you have any family?"

"No," the boy said. "I am all alone."

They took Johnny to the Brothers. Johnny never learned to read or write, but he was always full of joy. He never got upset and he made other boys forget their sadness or anger. He always had a funny song or dance to make them happy. Johnny loved to pray and attend Mass and he encouraged the other boys to go to with him. He loved God and felt that a smile and a happy voice would bring people closer to Him. Johnny Walker died at the age of eighteen when he fainted in a few inches of water and drowned. Brother Andrew said, "Johnny's a saint after a joyful, successful life if ever there was one."

In November 1964, Pope Paul VI (Pope John XXIII died in 1963) visited Bombay for the Eucharistic Congress. Millions of Indians lined the papal route for a glimpse of the Holy Father. Hindus believe they receive a special blessing called "darshan" by being in the presence of a holy person.

Mother Teresa left her Sisters' house to attend the Pope's welcoming ceremony, but she never arrived. On the street next to the palace where the ceremony was to take place, she found a dying couple under a tree. They were trying to help each other up, but both were too weak. Their faces were covered with blood and they were so thin, their bones poked through. Mother hurried to them, and took the man's hands in her own. She gave him a few words of comfort and he fell into her arms, dead. She laid him down under the tree, picked up his wife and put her on her shoulders. She carried the woman to Bombay's House of the Dying.

Mother Teresa did not make it to the opening ceremony to honor the Pope's visit, nor did she see Pope Paul VI arriving in the big white Lincoln Continental that the American people had given him. Pope Paul VI asked to see the poor sections of Bombay and was deeply moved when his escort told him about Mother Teresa and her Missionaries of Charity. "Before I leave our beloved India," he said, "I wish to do something to help Mother Teresa and her poor."

Mother was not even able to join the crowd gathered at the airport to say goodbye to the Pope. She was in the Home for the Dying caring for an old man who was taking his last breaths. The Pope gave his blessing to the large crowd and told them, "I am donating this white motorcar to Mother Teresa, Superior General of the Missionaries of Charity, to help her in her great work of love."

Mother never rode in that car. She raffled it off for half a million rupees. A poor widow who held the winning ticket gave the car to her son, but the car took so much gas he could not afford to drive it. When they were forced to sell the car, they gave half of the money to Mother Teresa. With the money, Mother was able to build a hospital for Shanti Nagar, the City of Peace. She had the main street in the town named Paul VI Avenue to show her gratitude to the Pope.

Young Agnes
Drawing by J.R. Roosenberg

Mother Teresa in 1960.

Mother Teresa with Dr. Anita Figueredo, Jordan, 1972.

CO-WORKERS OF MOTHER TERESA

LOVE TO PRAY –

feel often during the day
the need for prayer
and take trouble to pray.
Prayer enlarges the heart
until it is capable of containing
God's gift of Himself.
Ask and seek,
and your heart will grow
big enough to receive Him
and keep Him as your own.

God bless you
M. Teresa MC

Cover for the guidelines for the Co-Workers.

Mother Teresa with Jacqueline de Decker, 1982.

Mother Teresa with Jacqueline de Decker, 1993.

Mother Teresa's arrival at Lindbergh Field, San Diego, 1988.

Mother Teresa entering the hangar at Lindbergh Field, San Diego, 1988.

Mother Teresa greeting and blessing people in the hangar at Lindbergh Field, San Diego, 1988.

Mother Teresa laughing with friends; Maryanne Raphael in the background (right).

Mother Teresa in Tijuana, Mexico.

Mother Teresa in Tijuana, Mexico, 1989.

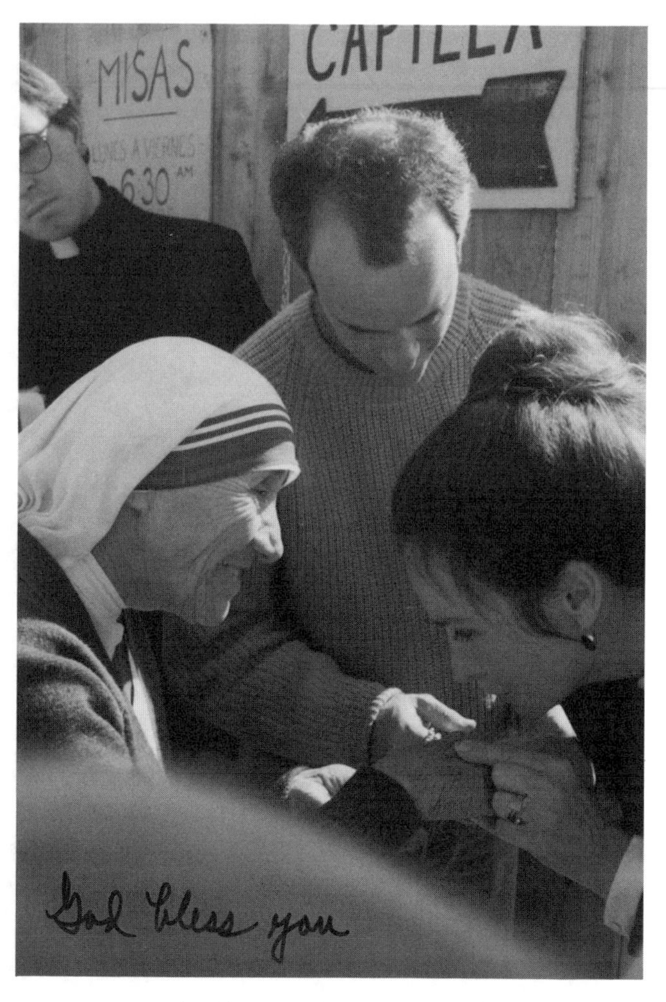

Mother Teresa in Tijuana, Mexico, 1989.

+
LDM

January 29, 1992
San Diego, CA

Dear Maryanne,

With deep appreciation I thank you for remembering me in your prayers.

My gratitude will be my prayer for you that you may become humble like Mary so as to become more and more like Jesus.

Together, let us thank God for all His tender love and care. He has been so good to me. The care that I received while in the hospital has been something great and beautiful. I am spoiled. Now that I have left the hospital and am feeling better, I ask you to pray much for China. We have been invited to bring Jesus to the people there who are hungering so much for God.

Continue to pray for me and my Sisters that we may not spoil God's work. Always be one heart full of love in the hearts of Jesus and Mary.

God bless you
M Teresa MC

A letter from Mother Teresa to Maryanne Raphael.

Mother Teresa at the
University of San Diego, 1992.

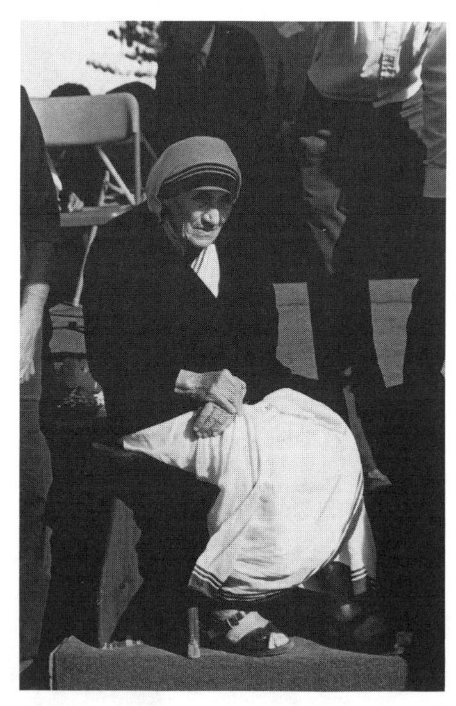

Mother Teresa in a moment of contemplation.

Mother Teresa in San Diego, 1996.

Buried in Albania

Mother Teresa was overjoyed when a Sister handed her a letter from her mother in Albania. Her hands shook as she tore open the envelope and began to devour the letter written in her beloved mother's familiar hand. "Thank you, God, for letting this letter reach me," she said. Her mother's handwriting was not as steady as usual and she noticed immediately that there were many sudden stops where the pen had slipped.

Mother Teresa could not pull her eyes away from the last lines of the letter: "I want to see you before I die. This is the only grace I ask of God, to see you and Lazar."

"Please, dear Jesus," she prayed, "You know how much she loves You. Please give her this last wish . . . " Then she forced herself to go on, ". . . if it is Your will, and if it isn't Your will, comfort her, let her feel Your loving presence."

Right away, Mother Teresa wrote Lazar. In his response, he said, "I promise you I will do everything in my power to get Mother and Aga back here." He reminded her that he had friends in high diplomatic posts who had promised to help him.

They received a reply from Albania: "Mrs. Drana Bojaxhiu and Miss Aga Bojaxhiu are not physically able to travel abroad at this time."

"If only there were some way one of us could go there," Lazar wrote. "I know it would be a great comfort to our dear mother."

"You work on one or both of us going to Albania," Mother wrote, "and I shall continue to try to get the two of them over here."

In July 1966, Mother Teresa made another trip to Venezuela to visit her Sisters and see about opening a house for the destitute. Eileen Egan accompanied her on her way back to Calcutta. They stopped off in Rome where Mother was to meet Lazar.

When Lazar saw Mother Teresa, he rushed to embrace her. Then he handed her a letter he had just received from Albania. It was from their sister Aga. She wrote, "Our beloved mother is dying of loneliness. She misses you two so. Her last wish is to visit you both. As for me, I am in good health although I too miss my brother and sister very much."

Lazar said angrily, "The Albanian officials lied. They are both being held prisoners. They are buried alive behind the iron curtain. We must get them out."

Mother Teresa and Eileen Egan went out looking for the Albanian Embassy in Rome, and finally found it in an old building that appeared deserted. Mother rang the doorbell repeatedly and prayed someone would arrive. After what seemed forever, a man opened the door. He looked amazed to find someone there. He stood there looking at the two women as though he were trying to decide in what language they would answer. Mother Teresa looked directly into his eyes and said in her original language, "I am from Albania." The man mumbled something in Albanian. Mother could not make it out, but she and Eileen assumed it was an invitation to enter the Embassy, so they followed him inside.

In spite of the fact that it was the middle of the day, the hall was so dark the women couldn't see anything. The man flipped on the electric lights and Mother Teresa saw that all the shutters were closed. She could now make out some overstuffed antique armchairs covered with muslin. Mother Teresa found herself wondering if her mother and her sister were living in the dark back in Tirana. The man sat down in one of the armchairs and motioned for Mother Teresa and her friend to do the same.

"I am Albanian," Mother repeated.

The man began to rattle off some long sentences in Albanian. They were so complicated and so rapid Mother could not make out anything he said. She attempted to say something else in Albanian, but the words completely escaped her. She blushed. "I've forgotten my own mother tongue," she told her friend. She felt helpless. "Blessed Mother, please give me the words I need." Then she heard herself asking, "Do you speak Serbo-Croatian?"

"I do," he said.

"I can't find the words in my childhood tongue," she began. "That was so long ago. You see, sir, my family is Albanian. Almost forty years ago, I went to India to become a Catholic nun. That was the last time I saw my mother and my sister. Now they are living in Tirana. I was christened Agnes Gonxha Bojaxhiu, but now everyone calls me Mother Teresa."

She was comfortable in Serbo-Croatian, and the man began to relax and listen to her story. He offered her coffee, but she explained the rule of her order that she was not to accept food or drink outside the convent.

"Tell me about your order," he said.

"We serve the poor in the streets of Calcutta. We are called the Missionaries of Charity because we are carriers of God's love."

The man's eyes inspected Mother Teresa, noting her inexpensive sari wrapped around her head, and her bare feet in well-worn sandals. He looked a bit puzzled.

Eileen Egan, who spoke Italian, told the man about the Home for the Dying and how the Missionaries of Charity gave free education to the poor.

Mother Teresa said trustingly, "I come here as a little girl trying to reach her mother, who is very ill."

Tears dropped from the man's eyes. He wiped his face with a white handkerchief.

"You see, my mother is eighty-one and hasn't seen me since I was eighteen. There is nothing I can do to get to my mother's side. I have tried everything I know. I must depend on you. Only the Albanian government can give me permission to go there or give her permission to come to Rome."

"I promise to do my best for you," the man said. "Come back here tomorrow at the same time. I will speak to the attaché for you."

"Thank you," Mother Teresa said. "I will be here."

The next day, the attaché was waiting for Mother Teresa. He began a conversation with her in Albanian, perhaps just to find out if she really was Albanian. She was able to answer him slowly, falteringly, searching for words that once were at the tip of her tongue and now lay deep in the hidden recesses of her psyche. She seemed to satisfy him that she was who she said she was. "I will get in touch with the government in Tirana and see what we can do for your mother and sister."

Later in the week, Mother Teresa returned to the Embassy. "I would like to speak with the attaché," she said.

"He is outside of Rome," a staff member told her.

"Have you any word about the exit visas?" Mother asked.

"We have no news of them," the man said.

"Where did the attaché go?" Mother asked.

"To Albania," the man replied. He did not invite her inside.

Mother Teresa was convinced the attaché would help her mother and sister once he got to Albania. She rushed to tell her brother Lazar the good news. In anticipation of their arrival, Lazar and Mother Teresa found a temporary home for Drana and Aga in Rome. They sent them a telegram to say they would meet them at the airport once they got their exit visas.

"You don't know how relieved I am," Lazar told Mother Teresa. "Look at this." He showed her an Italian newspaper. "This is what is going on in Albania. A priest was killed for baptizing a baby. He was Father Stephan Kurti, a distant relative of ours. Mosques, churches and temples have been demolished or are being used as warehouses. Can you imagine they are storing tin cans in the Cathedral? Religion is outlawed. You know how our dear mother and Aga must suffer."

"Thank God we will be seeing them soon," Mother said.

"And to think our beloved father died trying to free Albania from outside conquerors. He gave his life so that Albania would be independent. Now Albania is sovereign and her citizens are prisoners."

"We must pray for Albania," Mother Teresa said.

"The Albanians almost killed me too," Lazar continued. "When the Americans liberated Italy, I went to an American colonel and said, 'I am a colonel of a surrendered army. I would like to work for you.' He hired me to be his jeep driver and saved my life."

"Thank God you are still alive," Mother Teresa said. "You can help me with Mother and Aga."

There was still no word from the Albanian Embassy some weeks later when Mother Teresa left for Calcutta.

"Let me know as soon as you hear anything," Mother said hopefully.

"I really don't think we're ever going to hear anything from the Embassy," Lazar said gravely, "no good news anyway."

"All in God's time," Mother Teresa said.

She couldn't know then that she and Lazar would never again be with their beloved mother and sister on this earth.

A Work of Love

As a Society of Pontifical Rite, the Missionaries of Charity Sisters were now able to consider invitations from all over the world. On December 8, 1967, they opened a center in Colombo, Ceylon (today Sri Lanka). Colombo was the city Mother Teresa visited in 1928 when her ship from Ireland stopped there on the way to India.

Mother had never forgotten a family she had seen on the streets there gathered around a dead relative dressed in a red tattered loincloth. The entire family had seemed to be dying of starvation. Now she could do her part to help prevent similar situations.

In March 1968, Mother received a personal letter from Pope Paul VI. Before opening it, she slipped into the chapel. Her heart filled with joy as she read the Holy Father's words: "I would like you to open a house here in Rome, close to me. There is much poverty here." With the letter were two round-trip airplane tickets from Calcutta to Rome and a check for $10,000.

Mother wasted no time in getting to Rome to take a look at the situation. She took Sister Frederick with her. When they landed in Rome, a taxi driver offered to show them the famous monuments, but they wanted to see the worst slums. Instead, the papal emissary arrived and the Pope's limousine drove them directly to the Vatican. Pope Paul VI told her, "Mother Teresa, I'm so happy to see you here. I hope you will decide to open up a center near the Vatican."

"I am ready to open a house, Your Holiness, if there are poor people to be served." They rode around the poorer sections of the city and it did not take them long to see the desperate need that had prompted the Pope to invite them to open a center in the Eternal City. When they returned to the Vatican, Mother told the Pope, "Your Holiness, God seems to have left work for us to do just about everywhere."

On August 22, 1968, the anniversary of the opening of the House of the Dying, Nirmal Hriday, and the Feast of the Immaculate Heart of Mary, Mother Teresa brought a team of Indian Sisters to open a house in Rome.

The worst slums of Rome were in the outlying sections where the poor built shacks for themselves and their families. Many had no water, sewage disposal, or lights. Some beautiful pine trees and some impressive cypresses grew between the rows of shacks. Many of the inhabitants planted flowers and vines.

Mother Teresa brought her Sisters to the parish of San Stefano. They moved into a small house near the church and then into a little shack exactly like those in which their neighbors lived. They were only one block away from the ancient aqueduct that had once brought drinking water to the citizens of ancient Rome.

On May 4, 1969, four young novices changed their all-white sari for the blue bordered sari of the full-fledged Missionaries of Charity. Mother Teresa had a ceremony for them at San Stefano church. Friends and helpers from all over Rome gathered. Even Lazar was there.

The Rome foundation became the novitiate. After the ceremony, there was a reception in the largest room of the community center. The Cardinal attended as did several Monsignors and priests.

"Those young girls seemed so full of happiness as they surrendered their lives!" Lazar said, sounding surprised. Mother Teresa remembered what her brother had said about her "burying herself alive" if she became a nun. Perhaps now he was beginning to understand.

Lazar turned to Mother Teresa. "I did not know you before," he said. "It is only now that I come to know you."

Mother Teresa laughed. "You are still a boy."

"I want to ask you something, Mother Teresa," her brother said. "When I read those newspaper articles about you, I ask myself, 'Is it my sister saying these things?' How do you know what to say to all those people?"

"It comes to me at the time," Mother told him. "I just trust in the Holy Spirit to give me the words."

"What faith!" Lazar said. "What confidence! Frankly, I had very little faith left after I went away to school. One of my schoolmates went to Moscow where he became a firm Communist—Enver Hoxha—now, as you know, he's the head of Albania. None of the boys in my school were interested in religion. Most of them were atheists. It's no wonder my faith had begun to weaken!"

Several months later, at the airport in Rome, Lazar couldn't believe his eyes when he saw the "luggage" Mother Teresa and her Sisters were trying to check in. The Italian ground crew refused to load the bundles of tin cans and assorted clothing coming out of their wrappings of old newspaper and torn cardboard. Her brother was even more surprised when Mother Teresa and her Sisters knelt down and prayed right there in the middle of customs. Some other officials came to see what was happening. With a shrug, they agreed to take the bundles aboard.

"What were you doing?" Lazar asked his sister.

"Oh, we were just asking God to change the officials' minds," Mother answered.

Mother Teresa always tried to be on time for all her appointments. One day when she was on her way to meet with an important official at the Vatican, she stopped to talk with the poor. She found a weak old man living alone in a tiny shack. She washed him, talked with him and cleaned his home. Her driver became impatient and warned her, "Mother Teresa, you will be late." She did arrive late. Her Sisters said, "Only a very poor person could make Mother late for an appointment. The poor have top priority in her social calendar."

In March of 1969, Mother Teresa had come to Rome to prepare the Constitution for the new "International Association of Co-Workers of Mother Teresa." Mother chose the term "Co-Worker" for her helpers in honor of Mahatma Gandhi, who had called his own helpers Co-Workers.

Mother Teresa wanted to see that her helpers, or Co-Workers, worked in the same spirit as the Missionaries of Charity. "I do not want an auxiliary dedicated to raising funds and supplies," she told Patricia Kump, who was to become the first chairman for the United States. "What I want is a spiritual family united in their love for God as He shows Himself in His distressing disguise as the poorest of the poor."

Mother Teresa called Ann Blaikie and her husband John to Rome to help write some rules for the Co-Workers. For two days they worked steadily along with a German helper, Josepha Gosselke. Based on the idea that God can be served by serving His poor, the rules would instruct the Co-Workers all over the world how they must show their love for God by helping those in need. "Remember that many of the Co-Workers aren't Christians," Mother said. "For every Christian who helped me in India, I had nine non-Christians."

The Co-Workers often worked with the Missionaries of Charity Sisters and Brothers, and they had become the first lay organization made up of people of all faiths to be officially connected with a Roman Catholic order of nuns, priests and Brothers.

Ann and John Blaikie and Josepha Gosselke had the privilege of handing the regulations for the International Association of Co-Workers of Mother Teresa to the Holy Father. Pope Paul VI blessed all those who were present, the Missionaries of Charity and the Co-Workers all over the world. Mother Teresa told her Co-Workers, "We have to do the work that other people do not want to do. Many people will do the big things, but very few people will do the small things. So let us do little things with great love."

Although the Association of Co-Workers of Mother Teresa was now official, it remained very informal. They used mimeographed newsletters describing the work of the Sisters, Brothers and Co-Workers to keep in touch with one another. There were no dues. Co-Workers were asked to pray daily in union with the Missionaries of Charity the following prayers:

Make us worthy, Lord, to serve our fellow men throughout the world who live and die in poverty and hunger.
Give them, through our hands, this day their daily bread, and by our understanding love, give peace and joy.

Lord, make me a channel of Thy peace,
that where there is hatred, I may bring love;
that where there is wrong, I may bring the spirit of forgiveness;
that where there is discord, I may bring harmony;
that where there is error, I may bring truth;
that where there is doubt, I may bring faith;
that where there is despair, I may bring hope;
that where there are shadows, I may bring light;
that where there is sadness, I may bring joy.

Lord, grant that I may seek rather to comfort, than to be comforted;
to understand than to be understood;
to love rather than be loved;
for it is by forgetting self that one finds;
it is by dying that one awakens to eternal life.

These prayers were printed by the Co-Worker groups in different languages around the world. Mother asked that all meetings begin with prayer and that once a month Co-Workers unite for an hour of prayer.

Mrs. Ann Blaikie was named Chairman after Mother Teresa and Sister Frederick. Her title was soon changed to International Link. Jacqueline de Decker, who had helped Mother Teresa form the Sick and Suffering Links, was named International Link for the Sick and Suffering Co-Workers. Even though she herself was in constant pain, Jacqueline managed to travel to various countries to share the program, and she spent many hours joining Sick and Suffering Co-Workers with Missionaries of Charity. She wrote comforting letters to all those who confided in her.

Mother Teresa was always explicit that she did not want the Co-Workers to raise money for the work. "I don't want the Co-Workers ever to become a business," she said. "They must remain a way of life, a work of love."

"There is a tremendous strength growing in the world through this sharing together, praying together, suffering together, and working together," Mother told her Co-Workers. "We must pray the work. Do it for Jesus, to Jesus and through Jesus. By being faithful to our family, to the work God gives us, we help bring souls to Him. It is not how much we do that matters, but how much love we put into what we do."

Later in 1969, Archbishop James Robert Knox of Australia was concerned about the native people of his country. After visiting an Aboriginal reserve in New South Wales, Mother Teresa agreed to bring her Sisters there. A few days before she left for Australia, Mother fell out of her cot and broke her arm. The Sisters had to insist she see a doctor.

The doctor told her, "Mother Teresa, you can't travel with your arm in this condition."

"I have to go," Mother told him. So the doctor bound up the arm and most of her body. Traveling with all the bandages was so difficult that Mother Teresa asked one of the Sisters who was traveling with her to remove them. A little while later, the bone popped out of its setting. "Mother, you must see a doctor," the Sister said, looking at her arm.

"Never mind," Mother said. "Remember how I left for Venezuela after that accident in Darjeeling with my injured head."

Mother finally allowed the Sisters to get a doctor. With her arm in a cast, resting in a sling, she and the Sisters opened their house in the small town of Bourke, populated by Aborigines. It soon became a community center, where the Sisters taught classes in cooking and nutrition. They had sewing classes where the indigenous women learned to make curtains, bed covers and clothes. There was a room for the children where the Sisters taught religious education to Catholic children and tutored any child that asked for it with their schoolwork. Not far from the convent was the camp where many poor people lived. Huts were constructed of corrugated iron. Some had rust patches, and others were painted bright green or yellow. The Sisters obtained a large van for a school bus so they could drive the children from the camp to the public school. One of the Sisters drove the bus.

When Mother and five of her Sisters went to Melbourne, Australia, they found a neglected house with a leaking roof and a floor caked with dirt. "Well, we can start cleaning," Mother said after they had said a few prayers together to bless their new home. With the help of the Australian Co-Workers and some students, they cleaned the front room, prepared for Mass and made their beds. Since there were only five beds, one Sister slept under the table.

Because Mother Teresa still had a broken arm, the Sisters put some blankets on one side of her to protect it. After a hard day's work, the Sisters all slept soundly. When they woke up the next morning, they found all of the blankets spread over them to keep them warm during the cold night—Mother Teresa always put others' comfort before her own.

Next morning, the Sisters went into the streets in search of needy people. They came back with none. "There's no one living on the streets," they told Mother excitedly. Usually, no matter where they went in the world, they found homeless people. "Knock on the doors of the houses," Mother said. They went from door to door asking for ill people or others with immediate needs. The people of Melbourne thought the Sisters looked funny in their Indian clothes. It soon became obvious that the problems of Australia were not the same as those of India. The biggest challenge would be with drug addicts, alcoholics and those completely alone in the world. Mother told her Sisters, "I don't want you to do miracles in unsettling ways. I prefer you to make mistakes gracefully. If you do not seek to bring Christ to these people, you will be wasting your time and theirs."

The Sisters' work in Melbourne, and especially in Bourke, led to their being invited to open a house in Katherine in the Northern Territory. It was 2,000 miles away from Bourke but the needs were remarkably similar.

Something Beautiful for God

Mother Teresa met TV journalist Malcolm Muggeridge in 1968 when he interviewed her for the BBC. She had arrived late, and he was impatient. They began the television interview as soon as she entered the room. She held her Rosary tightly in her fingers throughout the interview and Malcolm was not particularly impressed by her haltingly simple answers to his questions; the producers thought the interview was so poor they planned a late-night showing of the program. It was eventually broadcast on a Sunday evening. Muggeridge couldn't believe the response that the interview received. The studio was flooded with letters and gifts of money for Mother's work. A second showing brought in even more letters and offerings.

Besides a documentary film about Mother Teresa filmed 1969 and released in 1970, Malcolm Muggeridge published the London edition of *Something Beautiful for God*, his book about Mother and her work in April of 1971. This was the book which turned the eyes of the world on Mother and her Missionaries of Charity.

Malcolm had long been known as an agnostic, and though he had recently come to know Jesus and had written a book called *Jesus Rediscovered*, he let it be known he was not interested in institutionalized religion. Mother was convinced that he would be filled with joy and peace if he joined the Catholic Church. He laughed at the idea and teased, "Mother Teresa, I hate to see you wasting all those prayers on me."

"Prayers are never wasted," she assured him. "Our Lord knows how to use them most proficiently."

They often went to Mass together and Malcolm would admit, "I do envy the peace and joy that Catholics seem to feel upon receiving the Eucharist but I just could not accept all that goes along with it."

"If it is His will, it will happen," Mother told him. "I will keep up my prayers for you."

Mother Teresa received many important awards and honors, but she was especially grateful to be chosen for the Pope John XXIII Peace Prize. On the evening of January 6, 1971, Mother and her Sisters got on the city bus to ride to the Vatican where Mother was to receive her award. All of the Sisters had tickets to get into the ceremony but Mother. She had given her ticket to a Sister who had none. When they reached the gate, one of the guards stopped Mother and said, "I'm sorry, but we cannot let you in without official permission." Mother Teresa did not know what to do. Just then a Bishop came along and stopped to congratulate Mother on being awarded the Peace Prize. The Sisters explained the problem to him. He told the guards, who asked for her forgiveness.

The entire diplomatic corps of the Vatican attended the award ceremony in formal dress. Mother Teresa's brother Lazar was there with his wife Maria and their daughter, Agi.

In presenting Mother Teresa the award, Pope Paul VI said, "Humble Mother Teresa, in whom we like to see the thousands and thousands of people dedicated full-time to the personal service of the most needy, becomes an example and symbol of the discovery, in which lies the secret of world peace, which we are all seeking. It is the discovery, ever so up-to-date, that man is our brother and she who comes to us as a Missionary of Charity is the apostle of brotherhood and the messenger of peace."

Mother said, "We will all make this year especially a year of peace. To this end we will try to speak more to God and with God and less to men and with men."

The $25,000 she received was used for the City of Peace Leprosy Foundation at Raigahr.

In the spring of 1971, West Pakistani troops invaded East Pakistan. About 250,000 refugees from East Pakistan flooded into Calcutta. The many differences between the Pakistanis of West and East Pakistan, divided by culture, ethnic origin and language, could no longer be solved by the fact that they shared a common religion, Islam.

Mother Teresa and her Missionaries moved into the midst of the most helpless victims, the children, the sick, the elderly and the wounded.

There was a large conference of Mother Generals of many Catholic congregations in Rome at the time. Mother Teresa flew to Rome and described the agony of her people. "There is danger of a cholera epidemic," Mother told them. Fifteen Sisters from various congregations offered to return with Mother immediately. She rushed with their passports to Indian authorities, who waived all regulations regarding missionaries to allow the Sisters to enter for emergency service. All of the Mother Generals stayed at the Mother House on Lower Circular Road with the Missionaries of Charity Sisters.

Many of the homeless refugees lived in the sewer pipes at Salt Lake. There were black, bloated corpses in open fields or by the roadside. Mother Teresa said, "India has been wonderful in accepting and taking care of millions of Pakistani refugees and we in India will continue to care for them. In opening the door to them, the Indian Prime Minister, Mrs. Gandhi, has done a wonderful Christ-like thing."

An appeal booklet was distributed around the world quoting Mother: "Let us remember this, the people of Pakistan, the people of India, the people of Vietnam, all people wherever they may be are the children of God, all created by the same hand. Today the Pakistani refugees belong to us in a special way. The problem is not only India's. It is the world's problem. We have millions of children suffering from malnutrition and starvation. Unless the world provides food and proteins, these children will die and the world will have to answer for their death."

Mother and her Missionaries cleaned the hospital tents for those with dysentery, cholera, smallpox and other deadly diseases. The whole world responded with food, medicine, tents, building materials, trucks and volunteers.

In December 1971, the Indian army entered East Pakistan, and on December 16th, the troops of West Pakistan surrendered. East Pakistan declared itself independent of West Pakistan and changed its name to Bangladesh.

Mother Teresa and some of her Sisters were on one of the first truck convoys to enter Bangladesh after the two-week war ended. The first thing they did was bury the many dead bodies they found lying everywhere. In one town, the authorities offered Mother and her Sisters a huge building for their work. Mother thanked them and said, "I think it is better for us to work in smaller, plainer houses. The people feel more at home."

An estimated 200,000 women had been raped. Many very young girls were pregnant. In their culture a woman who had been raped would never find a husband and they saw their young lives as ruined. Some of them committed suicide. Mother Teresa opened a house for raped and pregnant women in a 300-year-old convent in old Dacca. Sheikh Majuibur Rahman, leader of the new nation, said, "We need to recognize the sacrifices of the women who have been violated by the enemy. These women should be considered heroines of the nation." Many of the pregnant women, especially the very young, wanted abortions. Mother begged them to have the babies and give them to her. "The Sisters will take care of you and we will find a good home for the babies."

Mother had hoped to open a house in New York City early in 1971, but the problems in Bangladesh had kept her occupied. Finally, in September, five Indian Sisters arrived at Kennedy airport with their bedrolls and cardboard boxes of Indian kitchen utensils.

The Handmaids of Mary in Harlem arranged sleeping quarters for the five

Sisters. On October 14th, when Mother arrived, her Missionaries of Charity were waiting for her. They rushed under the restraining ropes to greet Mother Indian style with a crepe paper wreath they had made for her. Mother patted each Sister on her forehead and gave them her blessing.

Mother Teresa was with the Sisters for only a short time before she left for Washington D.C. to recieve an award at a special conference on mental retardation sponsored by the Joseph P. Kennedy Jr. Foundation. Senator Edward Kennedy, whom Mother had met in Bangladesh, was the Foundation's president and had requested Mother's presence. Rosemary Kennedy, Senator Kennedy's sister, was mentally retarded and her family was turning this apparent tragedy into compassionate service for others. The Foundation had already spent $42,000,000 on research into the prevention and care of mental retardation.

At the conference, Mother Teresa watched a movie made in a Baltimore hospital where a newborn baby with Down's syndrome had been allowed to die by starvation. When the film ended, Mother exclaimed, "Court order or no court order, I would have snatched up that baby and run with him to a safe place where he could be saved. I wouldn't care if the police came after me. I wouldn't give up that baby."

As if to punctuate this point, a section of Malcolm Muggeridge's film "Something Beautiful for God" was shown, the scene where Mother looks at a dying baby and says joyfully, "There's life in her!"

Senator Edward Kennedy then presented Mother Teresa with the John F. Kennedy Memorial Award. He said, "My mother, Mrs. Rose Kennedy, wanted to present this award, but she is not well enough to be with us." As he handed her the award, he told the crowd, "In her unique geography of compassion, Mother Teresa knows where the need is and in her unique faith never doubts that the means to meet it, in help and material resources, will be forthcoming. It is our privilege to ensure that her faith is ever more abundantly fulfilled."

The award was $12,000, a silver-based Waterford crystal vase, and a crystal plate with an image of the Archangel St. Raphael and a note that read: "Seraph Raphael, chief of the guardian angels who protect and guide mankind, to honor knowledge as the servant of compassion and love."

Mother bowed deeply in her Indian salute and said, "Thank you. God bless you." The audience gave her a standing ovation.

That evening, Mother Teresa met Andrew Young, who had worked with Dr. Martin Luther King Jr. in his nonviolent campaigns for civil rights in the United States. He told Mother how Dr. King's work had been strongly inspired by the suffering Jesus and by Gandhi's peaceful resistance. Mother eagerly invited him to visit with her and the Sisters in Harlem. The very next evening, Andrew Young was at the door of the Harlem convent of the Handmaids of Mary. Mother Teresa invited him into the parlor and said, "Please tell me about the beautiful things in the lives of American blacks."

"Well, Mother Teresa. Religion plays an important part in the lives of the black people of the South. We love to sing and praise the Lord as part of our worship."

"Could you sing one of the hymns for me?" Mother asked. His deep, rich voice belted out "Lead, Kindly Light," which had been one of Mahatma Gandhi's favorite songs. Mother's clear soprano joined in. Not long after that, Andrew Young became the first black Congressman from Georgia, then U.S. Ambassador to the United Nations, and then mayor of Atlanta.

When she was feeling better, Mrs. Rose Kennedy made a personal gift to increase Mother's award from $12,000 to $15,000.

Mother gave the Waterford crystal vase to Sister Andrea, saying, "This will go toward turning the Dum Dum refugee center into a permanent center for retarded and handicapped children. I will call it the Nirmala Kennedy Center."

Shortly after that, the Sisters found their own place in the South Bronx and moved out of the Handmaids of Mary's convent. When Mother went to inspect the site before the Sisters moved in, she found it was a three story building that had previously housed the Sisters who had taught at St. Pius X's Catholic school. Mother loved its simplicity. Right away she chose the chapel and had Christ's last words from the Cross, "I THIRST," printed on the wall behind the altar, to remind all of the visitors of Jesus' great thirst for souls. She told her Sisters, "Nothing in the world is more important than bringing souls to Jesus. That is what our work is all about."

"You can use the convent temporarily, Mother," a workman told her, "but all of the remaining buildings on this block are scheduled for demolition." Mother learned that many had been destroyed by arsonists and those that remained seemed ready to collapse on their own.

The American edition of the book *Something Beautiful for God* was published in New York in October 1971. Author Malcolm Muggeridge and Mother Teresa appeared on the David Frost Show, the Today Show (where Barbara Walters interviewed them), and several other television shows.

Whenever Mother appeared in public, she believed it was a chance to save souls. She accepted honors mainly as a gift to the donors, a chance for them to recognize Jesus in the poorest of the poor and in themselves.

When Mother agreed to receive awards and make speeches, she was trying to get her work known in order to raise awareness about the poor. She never depended on the world's wealth to care for her poor. She said, "I accept awards in the name of the poorest of the poor. I believe that when awards are given to me the existance of the poor in the world is being recognized." She wanted the rich to meet the poor, to love them and to see their beauty and learn that dignity and honor do not come from riches, but from love, forgiveness and compassion.

Many felt this love and compassion and were moved by it.

One such person was Senator Edward Kennedy, chairman of the Committee on Refugees of the United States Senate, who went with Mother to the Salt Lake and the Center near Dum Dum Airport in Calcutta. He later told of his personal experiences and remarked, "You see children with legs and feet swollen with edema (fluid retention) and malnutrition, you see babies going blind for lack of vitamins or covered with sores that never heal. Most difficult of all, you see the corpse of the child who died just the night before. I have a collection of personal observations that really burned my soul."

Another was Jerry Brown, former governor of California, who spent three weeks helping Mother in Calcutta.

Daphne Rae, the wife of the headmaster of Westminster, one of Britian's oldest schools, joined Mother in Calcutta and worked with her. She wrote a book about her experiences called *Love Until it Hurts*.

It was on the behalf of persons like these that Mother Teresa often prayed, like St. Paul, "Lord let there be less of me and more of thee."

Mother Teresa told her Missionaries of Charity and her Co-Workers many times: "The hardest thing for me is public appearances. It is easier to clean a leper's wounds. So I made an agreement with the Lord. Each time I appear in public one soul is released from Purgatory."

Later, when Mother received the Nobel Peace Prize, a Co-Worker said, "Well, Mother, it looks like you've cleaned out Purgatory."

Mother laughed and said, "It doesn't take Purgatory long to get filled up again."

When, in 1972, Mother Teresa received a telegram from her brother Lazar in Palermo, Italy, she knew something was terribly wrong. Tears clouded her eyes as she read: "Pray for Mother, who died on July 12th."

Lazar and Mother Teresa had tried every possible way to get their mother and sister out of Albania. President John F. Kennedy, French President General Charles de Gaulle, Secretary General of the United Nations U Thant, Indira Gandhi, and others had tried to help, but none of them could open the iron curtain long enough to allow even a brief visit. Later, Mother Teresa learned that even if she'd obtained a visa there was a good chance she would have never been allowed to leave Albania as long as it remained Communist. Mother was torn between her desire to see her beloved family and her call to serve Jesus in the world. In the end, as much as it tortured her, she put her mother and sister in God's hands and stayed outside, continuing her work.

Mother told her brother, "Up until now I have succeeded in obtaining everything with love and prayer. But there are still barriers and obstacles that not even love can break down. All she ever asked for was to see us just once more."

Mother went directly to the chapel where she spent the afternoon in prayer. Later she said, "She is His more than mine. Our sacrifice, hers and mine, of not seeing each other has obtained much strength for the work and it has brought us closer to God."

Her sister Aga was now all alone in Albania. She had given up marriage in order to take care of her ill mother; now she herself was ill and there was no one to care for her. She would die in Tirana on August 25, 1973.

Mother Teresa, who went all over the world to help those in need, was unable to help her own family.

Globalization

In 1971, while Mother Teresa was in England opening a house, she sent a team of Sisters to Northern Ireland to see if there was anything they could do to improve relationships between Catholics and Protestants there. Northern Ireland had been a hotbed of violence and terrorism for years as an underprivileged Catholic minority struggled with Protestent extremists for equal rights, and the outlawed Irish Republican Army sought independence from Great Britain, whose troops were an ever-present deterrent. Bombings in the neighborhood pubs killed hundreds. Mother called together some 400 Co-Workers in Dublin. "I want to open a Missionaries of Charity house in Belfast," she said.

"Mother, that's the most dangerous part of the country," one Co-Worker blurted out.

"Yes, I know," Mother said. "That's why we must go there."

Mother and four Sisters arrived in the war-torn city of Belfast, with bedrolls and a violin. They went to the Catholic town of Ballymurphy and moved into a house in which a priest had recently been murdered. The house had been stripped of everything by vandals and was empty. The Sisters cleared away the debris and made it habitable.

Hatred was everywhere. Even the sermons were sometimes full of hate. The Sisters helped widows whose husbands had been killed in the fighting, mothers who had lost sons and oftentimes husbands, too, who were left alone with little ones to raise.

"The Irish have always believed in the sacredness of life," Mother said. "Don't ever allow that belief to die out. And the Irish have always loved the Rosary and community prayer. The Irish have given many missionaries to the world. Don't be unfaithful now. Many years ago I came from Yugoslavia to enter the order of the Sisters of Our Lady of Loreto, in Rathfarnham, Ireland. That is my small connection with the Irish people and their beautiful missionary spirit. But perhaps it isn't so small because in Ireland I learned to love God and to serve him faithfully. My gratitude to the Irish people springs from that."

Mother had wanted her own nuns to work alongside of a small group of Anglican nuns, but she soon realized they were not wanted. Although leaving Belfast was a great sacrifice, Mother Teresa would later consider it "fruitful" since afterward the same nuns who'd left would give themselves to the suffering of others.

Mother Teresa was getting so many requests for her Missionaries of Charity to open houses, she had to choose her locations with great care. One such place was Ethiopia, where she would investigate the possibility of reaching those in the grip of starvation because of a great drought.

Another was Gaza in Israel, where, in 1973, displaced Palestinians and Israeli Jews fought over territory. Once more Mother's Sisters arrived just after a priest (Father Hana Nimry) was murdered. His home was given to the Sisters. It was not far from the Gaza Strip where 400,000 refugees struggled to survive. Here too the Sisters had to clean up bloodstains from the floor. Soon the Sisters had made friends with the children, the sick and the elderly, and their days were filled with prayer, service, and moments of love, laughter and tears with the poor.

Mother's work of helping those in peril was also carried out by The Missionaries of Charity Brothers who went where they were most needed. Brother Andrew, their Servant General, left India in 1973. He went to Saigon and decided to bring a team of Brothers to Vietnam to see what they could offer this troubled land, where a long civil war pitted the Communist North against the American-supported South. Right away, they began a House of Hospitality for widows with young children and women who had been living with soldiers and were now disowned by their own families and unable to find work. The Missionaries of Charity Brothers did not set out to do any particular work, but they tried to create an atmosphere where people could grow and love and be what God wanted them to be.

One day a rickshaw drew up in front of the house and out stepped an attractive young Vietnamese woman named My Le with three young children. Homeless and without a husband, she had become a prostitute to support herself and her children. When she gave up prostitution, her only hope was her parents, but they let her down. She was now desperate for a home and food. The Brothers took her and her children in and they soon became the heart of the House of Hospitality.

The house kept growing until finally there were more than sixty people living there. The little community was very supportive of one another and they began to rely on the Brothers less and less.

In 1974 the Brothers moved to Phnom Penh, Cambodia, where there was more need. The Khmer Rouge, a Communist movement led by Pol Pot, was fighting to gain control of Cambodia. They eventually did, and during the struggle and its aftermath, huge numbers of Cambodians were murdered, worked to death, or killed by starvation.

The Brothers would lie in bed at night listening to rockets. They could feel the ground rumble beneath them. Every town and every building along Highway Four of Phnom Penh had been destroyed for over thirty miles. Most of the survivors were in refugee camps. The Brothers opened a Hospitality House for the refugees and, when their first house was full, they opened a second. By 1975 Brother Andrew decided it was not right to keep the young Brothers in such a dangerous situation with the war accelerating each day. None of them wanted to leave, but they had taken a vow of obedience and they all agreed to go, except one. Brother Brian Walsh, a twenty-three-year-old American Missionary of Charity, told Brother Andrew, "I can't go. I have to stay here with the Cambodian people that I've grown to love."

"Please come with us," Brother Andrew begged.

"I'm so sorry, Brother Andrew, I have to stay here."

Two of the Brothers considered taking him by force when they were leaving, but Brother Brian slipped away and was last seen with some French Benedictine monks. The Brothers got out just in time, for the Khmer Rouge occupied Phnom Penh and soon North Vietnam took over Saigon.

When Brother Andrew saw that everyone was evacuated except for Brother Brian, he himself decided to stay. He went from one Hospitality House to the next doing whatever he could. Within a short time the Khmer Rouge had taken over all the houses, and the people were homeless once more.

Each day a new list of foreigners to be deported was posted, and at last Brother Andrew's name was on it. He looked at the city the night before he left and he wept. "I shall never be the same again, and I know that I shall have an ache in my heart for these people until the day I die."

In time, 2,000,000 perished in Cambodia. Brother Brian was presumed dead. Brother Andrew, Brother Michael and Brother Gary all wrote to Brother Brian's mother. She shared one of her son's last letters with them: "I hope you are at peace. Even if this is wrong, staying on here, I know that God can make it up to you a hundred times over. I don't believe I'm doing anything wrong. But I have a lot of peace that I know belongs to you as much as it does to me. We must think of the words: 'There is no greater love than to lay down one's life for one's friends.'"

In June 1975, the Vatican asked Mother Teresa to be its representative at the World Conference of the International Women's Year held on the thirtieth anniversary of the United Nations in Mexico City. The gathering was a gala event with women from some 125 different countries. Mother Teresa attended all the meetings, listened to the formal speeches, and she took part in workshop sessions on development. Many speakers stressed that peace is necessary for equality and progress.

Mother Teresa introduced the Pope's resolution entitled "Women in Poverty." It began by saying that poverty limits the enjoyment of basic human rights and creates powerlessness and lack of hope. It urged all women to have a special concern for poor and disadvantaged women on whom poverty places particularly crushing burdens. It ended by asking women who have some material comforts to work with poor and disadvantaged women, sharing in their daily struggle to improve their living conditions. The resolution was adopted and appeared in the final report of the Mexican Conference.

As soon as there was a break, Mother went to visit the little colonial church with the baptismal font where Juan Diego was baptized. Juan Diego was the Aztec Indian to whom Our Lady of Guadalupe, the Patroness of Mexico, appeared in 1531. She also wanted to see the poor people of the city and found someone to take her on a tour. She saw that the poor people lived in homemade shacks, sometimes with eight or nine children. But the Mexicans had a strong sense of family and a great hope for the future.

During her talk at the Conference, Mother Teresa mentioned Father Miguel Augusta Pro, a Jesuit priest during the Mexican Revolution who gave Last Rites and said Mass secretly. When a professor at the University of Mexico asked Mother Teresa what she would like to see in the city, she said, "Father Pro's grave." He led her to the spot at the National Lottery Building where Father Pro had been shot by a firing squad on November 23, 1927. Then he took her to the cemetery where the priest was buried, and she knelt in silent prayer.

Mother had returned to her hotel when the phone rang and a man said, "President Echeverria wants to see you before you leave Mexico, Mother. He will send his limousine for you."

"I will be happy to meet the President but I have an appointment this evening with Jose Chavez, editor of a Catholic monthly magazine, and I don't want to miss it." Chavez wanted Mother to meet a group of local Catholics interested in her work and what they could do to help.

Later that day, when Mother was seated next to the President, he asked, "What is the meaning of this sari you wear?"

"I chose it because it was the way our poor women in India dress," she carefully explained. "We wear it at all times." She explained that the Missionaries of Charity Sisters were Catholic nuns in the traditional sense.

Then President Echeverria said, "Mother, I would like to invite you to bring your

Sisters to Mexico."

She thought about Father Pro, who had given his life for the Catholic faith in Mexico when it was forbidden. "Thank you, Mr. President," Mother said. "But since ours is a religious society, the invitation to come to Mexico must come from the head of the local church."

"I am certain that can be arranged," the President said. "I am truly concerned about the poor people of Mexico and I know your Sisters will be a great help to us."

"It is all in God's hands," Mother said.

"I personally will see that your Sisters get everything they need to begin the work," the President promised.

The President's wife brought some of their eight children to meet Mother Teresa. As Mother was leaving, Mrs. Echeverria handed her a small lacquered cross and said, "I would like you to have this as an example of the fine work done by our poor people." Mother left the President and his wife in time to keep her appointment with Mr. and Mrs. Jose Chavez in their home.

The Cardinal of Mexico City sent an invitation to Mother Teresa a short time later, and the following year a team of Missionaries of Charity Sisters arrived in Mexico City. President Echeverria gave them a vehicle to help them with their work. Mother and her Sisters chose a simple hut by the city dump as their home.

By October 1975, Mother Teresa was back in Calcutta in time for a week-long celebration of the Silver Jubilee, the 25th anniversary of the founding of her Missionaries of Charity. She asked the people of Calcutta to help her give thanks with prayer services in their own denominations. During the week she received responses from the Hindus, Buddhists, Catholics, Muslims, Jains, Jews, Sikhs, Armenians, Assembly of God, and the Methodist and Mar Thomas Syrian churches.

Mother Teresa recited the Magnificat, the Jewish maiden's prayer, in the Moghen David Synagogue. "For He that is mighty hath done great things to me; And Holy is His name . . . He hath filled the hungry with good things; And the rich He hath sent empty away. He hath received Israel, His servant, Being mindful of His Mercy; As He spoke to our fathers, to Abraham and to his seed forever." The chief rabbi took Mother Teresa and her Sisters into the Holy of Holies after the services to show them the scrolls of the prophets.

Mother took a different group of professed Sisters and third year novices to each religious celebration. It may have been a historical first, so many spiritual paths united together in thanksgiving. Mother's instructions to all the religious groups were: "Simplicity. No expenses, no concerts, no decorations, only thank you to

God." She wanted all attention to be on God. "It is His work, not ours."

From their small beginnings of twelve Missionaries of Charity, the group now had 1,133 members living all around the world. In India, they had houses in Calcutta, Andhra Pradesh, Bihar, Gujarat, Haryana, Kerala, Meghalaya, Madhya Pradesh, Maharashtra, Mysore, Orissa, Tamil Nadu, Uttar Pradesh, Union Territories, and West Bengal. Outside India were houses in Africa, Australia, Bangladesh, Europe, Mauritius, the Middle East, Papua New Guinea, the United States, and South America.

At the Jain Temple, Mother Teresa and her Sisters sat near Jain nuns in white saris. In the far corner near the worship stand sat Jain monks who wore no clothes, practiced celibacy, nonpossession, fasting, and mortification. Mother Teresa was moved by a Jain nun who pulled out her hair one piece at a time as a form of penance. Her head was covered with blood but she did not utter a sound. Mother felt compelled to do the same thing, so she reached under her veil and pulled out some of her own hair to feel in union with the nun.

October 2nd was the late Mahatma Gandhi's birthday. Mother Teresa was glad to include his memory in the Silver Jubilee celebration. On the 106th anniversary of Gandhi's birth, the Leprosy Rehabilitation Center at Titagarh, which had been run by the Sisters, was turned over to the Missionaries of Charity Brothers and renamed Gandhiji Prem Nivas (Gandhi Center of Love).

On October 4th, Mother and her Sisters were at the Hindu Temple of Shree Lakshmi Narayan. Everyone touched Mother's feet. The priest and all present invoked the thousand names of God with great devotion in solemn Sanskrit.

When October 7th arrived, the Sisters from all over Calcutta gathered at the Mother House on Lower Circular Road for a Mass at 6:30 in the morning. Mother was surrounded by most of the women who had joined her twenty-five years earlier. Sisters Agnes, Dorothy, Margaret Mary, Bernard, Florence, Clare, and Francesca were there. Sister Gertrude was in Yeman and Sister Laetitia in Papua New Guinea. The Mass was celebrated by Archbishop Picachy with those priests who had served as chaplains to the Sisters. Among them were Father Edward Le Joly and Father Celest Van Exem. Father Julian Henry had been invited but he did not like public ceremonies and had promised to thank God in private. Michael Gomes, Mother's original landlord and helper, served the Mass. His wife and daughter Mabel, who had often gone with Mother Teresa into the slums, were there also. Brother Andrew was present with some of his Missionaries of Charity Brothers. In the front row were some of the survivors from the House of the Dying, who had been rescued twenty-five years earlier. The Sisters called them "our most precious gift." The hymns sung at that Mass had been mimeographed and sent to Sisters in 61 houses all over India and to 27 houses scattered all over the world.

Later that week, Mother Teresa managed to slip away from the celebrations to visit the Gomes house at 14 Creek Lane, where it had all begun. Michael Gomes was astonished when he opened the door and found Mother Teresa standing there. "Mother Teresa! What a beautiful surprise!"

"I just wanted to remember the beginning," Mother said with a smile.

"Of course, Mother."

"I wanted to thank you once more, Michael, for all your help."

"Thank you, Mother, for all the love and inspiration you have given to me and to my family."

"I want you and your family to have this," Mother said, handing him the beautiful picture of Our Lady that had hung over the altar in the upper room from the time of the beginning of her work there.

"God bless you, Mother," Michael Gomes said, holding the picture with great reverence and love.

"God bless you and your family," Mother said. "And now I must get back to my sisters."

A week after the Jubilee, Mother Teresa left Calcutta for New York to participate in a Spiritual Summit Conference of the Temple of Understanding to celebrate the thirtieth anniversary of the United Nations. The other speakers represented Buddhism, Judaism, Islam, and Hinduism.

When she left New York, Mother was whisked off to Washington D.C. where she had been chosen to speak on Peace at a sequel to the International Women's Year Conference in Mexico. Margaret Mead was speaking on equality. When Margaret Mead was introduced to Mother Teresa, she took Mother's hand and kissed it.

Before she returned to Calcutta, Mother Teresa met with Dr. Elizabeth Kubler-Ross, who had been working with dying patients for many years and had written a best-selling book, *Death and Dying*. Dr. Kubler-Ross wanted to hear about Mother Teresa's Home for the Dying at Kali's temple. They shared with one another their experiences with the dying and their recognition of the need for personal loving care for them. Mother told her, "For me that is the greatest development of human life, to die in peace and in dignity, for that's eternity." She explained to Dr. Kubler-Ross that most of the people who died at her Home for the Dying in Calcutta were Hindu or Muslim. "We don't try to convert them to Christianity but to bring them closer to

God, to make them better Hindus or Muslims or Christians or whatever their religion. And all of them have died beautiful deaths. We say we are giving them a ticket to St. Peter and they all like that."

Dr. Kubler-Ross told Mother Teresa, "Most of my work has been an effort to help the person who is dying to feel a part of the living so that they are not isolated and lonely. The regimented impersonality of modern hospitals has led me to recommend the Hospice movement for the care of the dying. They need a loving, supportive environment where pain is controlled or prevented along with any unpleasant symptoms."

"Yes," Mother agreed. "My prayer is that before they die, all people will know that they are loved."

The Contemplatives

Mother Teresa was invited to deliver the opening statement at a two day Habitat Forum, sponsored by the United Nations. It was in Vancouver, Canada on May 31, 1976. The topic was "Improving the Quality of Life for the Handicapped in the World's Settlements." "We feel you are the foremost spokesperson in the world for the poor and the handicapped," the organizers said.

Mother's Habitat Forum talk took place in a hangar, part of a former army barracks. On the upper benches, young people in jeans and long flowered dresses sat singing. Up front sat special guests in wheelchairs, many with their necks in metal braces. There was also a section for those who were deaf and dumb.

Mother began her talk with the prayer, "Lord, make us worthy to serve the poor around the world who live and die in poverty and hunger." As she spoke, a young woman translated the words into sign language with rapid, graceful movements.

"We are all handicapped in one way or another," Mother said. "Sometimes it can be seen on the outside; sometimes it is on the inside." After she finished her talk, Mother shook hands with each person in a wheelchair and with all the people in the seats for the deaf and dumb. She thanked the young woman for translating her words into sign language. Then the young people surrounded her. Mother Teresa had not asked for donations, but someone had put a large garbage can near the podium. It was filled with gifts and a total of over $4,000.

Between public appearances, Mother Teresa visited many convents and found a sad situation facing many orders. Young women were not joining and the present Sisters were growing too old to work and there was no money to support them. Mother expressed concern and promised to pray for them.

Lady Barbara Ward, noted author and leader in the causes of peace, justice and environmental protection, was also a forum speaker. She had great admiration for Mother's work although she had never met her before. Mother was happy to learn that she and Barbara were staying in the same convent. After publishing many books on economic justice and protecting the earth such as *The Home of Man* and *Spaceship Earth*, Barbara had decided to focus her efforts on the need for pure water.

"Pure water is a special need for the poorest of the poor who drink nothing but water and who often run the risk of dying due to impure drinking water," Barbara told Mother, who quickly agreed.

"Millions of people die because of diseases coming from impure water and I want the United Nations, governments and social agencies to start a campaign so that people, especially the poor, will have access to pure drinking water by 1990. I believe clean water will eliminate about 30% of the most desperate problems of humanity."

"You are right," Mother Teresa told her. "Bad water causes many problems for the poor."

Barbara became very serious. "May I ask you a question, Mother?"

"Of course," Mother said.

"Do you think working for pure water is an adequate justification for the rest of my life? I have cancer, you know, and I don't know how much time I have left, but I want to use it for something worthwhile."

"It is a beautiful cause," Mother told her. "And it is a special gift being chosen to lead that struggle for the very poor."

Over lunch, Barbara Ward, Bishop James Carney and Mother Teresa discussed the dangers from various types of technology, especially nuclear. Barbara emphasized the moral problems, unchecked greed and consumerism. "These days when the earth is in danger, we must ask ourselves what the Son of Man means." Mother Teresa said, "People can feel close to Jesus because He is like them, the Son of Man."

When the Bishop brought his car to take Mother Teresa to the Pacific Coliseum in Vancouver for her next speech, he seemed a little nervous. "You know, Mother Teresa, there wasn't enough time to publicize your talk. I don't know what kind of crowd we will have. Filling a big coliseum isn't easy, you know." When they arrived the houselights were dark, and the Bishop led Mother directly to the auditorium towards the stage. The houselights were turned on and a blinding spotlight shone on Mother. Backstage, the choir began singing, "Lord, make me a channel of your peace; where there is hatred, let me sow love . . ."

The Bishop smiled broadly. The Coliseum was filled to capacity, with people standing in the back.

Mother began her talk. "Jesus made Himself the Bread of Life, to make sure we understand what He is saying, to satisfy our hunger for Him, to satisfy our love for Him. Even that is not enough for Him. So He makes Himself the Hungry One, so we can satisfy His hunger for our love. And by caring for the poor with love, we are satisfying His hunger for our love."

As she finished, a small dark-haired boy in a traditional Native American costume came towards Mother bringing her a gift, a hand-carved totem topped with an eagle's head.

"My name is Eagle Bear," the boy said. "And I speak for the Native North

American people. We are the original people of Vancouver."

A Catholic Sister who was sitting with the Native North Americans shouted, "We all love you, Mother Teresa!" and the words echoed throughout the Coliseum.

That afternoon, back in the convent, Barbara Ward told Mother, "I would like to be one of your Co-Workers." Mother Teresa welcomed her.

Later on, Barbara wrote to Mother: "Thank you for making me a Co-Worker. We are getting great support for the idea of clean water by 1990. I still have pleurisy (getting better), but there are no firm promises on the progress of my cancer treatment. So perhaps I am to work. Or perhaps I am to be ill. But as you say, it is God's way whatever it is. It is a wonderful privilege to feel that anything I am able to do can be united with your work and pushed forward by your prayers. Your loving letter made me feel very happy. I will try now to think of nothing but doing God's will in whatever form He presents it to me. Your loving child, Barbara."

Barbara once told Mother, "I would love to spend my last days with you in Calcutta." But like Jacqueline de Decker, Barbara had to give up the idea of being an active Co-Worker and instead became a Sick and Suffering Co-Worker for the last five years of her life.

Mother Teresa told her, "When the time comes and we cannot pray, it is very simple to let Jesus pray in us to the Father, in the silence of our hearts. If we cannot speak, He will speak for us. If we cannot pray, He will pray for us. So let us give Him our inability and our nothingness. He will put them to great use."

On the afternoon of August 1, 1976, Mother Teresa was in Philadelphia for the Eucharistic Congress. Philip Scharper, a well-known editor, interviewed her on a television program that was broadcast throughout the United States.

"Would you please tell us, Mother Teresa, just what it is you and your Sisters do?"

"We give the dying tender love and care; everything possible that the rich get for their money we give the poor for the love of God."

As the interview ended, he asked, "Do you have a message for the people of the United States, Mother?"

"If the people of the United States do not answer the needs of other people, they will miss the touch of Christ in their lives. What is given to them is given to share, not to keep." The theme of the Eucharistic Congress was the physical and spiritual hunger of humanity. At the opening of the session, Mother Teresa seemed to represent the hungry of the world. She stood over a table of round loaves, recited a prayer, then broke the bread and shared it. A morsel of bread was shared with as many people as possible in the crowd of over 6,000 people gathered in the Civic Center auditorium.

This Congress brought together Mother Teresa and Don Helder Camara, Archbishop of Olianda-Recife, Brazil, another famous friend of the poor. While he was making his speech, Don Helder looked over at Mother Teresa and said, "I want to pause now and kiss the two hands of Mother Teresa." He walked over to where she was sitting, took her hands, kissed them and returned to the podium.

Don Helder spoke of institutionalized violence and the need to build new structures to eliminate oppression and bring justice to the very poor. He explained how Martin Luther King Jr.'s methods of nonviolence could be used. "There are those who feel that building these new structures is the only task that matters, and helping the poor comes second. I agree we need new structures but in the meantime . . . " He looked directly at Mother Teresa. "In the meantime, the hunger of the poor cries out for those who will feed and help them."

300 theologians and leaders of religious groups discussed the meaning of the Eucharist meal. When they asked Mother Teresa for her comments, she asked all of them to pray together.

A Mass for Freedom and Justice was celebrated that evening by Cardinal Karol Wojtyla of Kracow (who later became Pope John Paul II) with 400 concelebrants. As darkness fell, the people lit candles and sang hymns.

One evening, before a prayer service, there was a foot-washing ceremony during which Mother Teresa washed the feet of a Mennonite man.

Because the crowds were trying to get close to Mother Teresa, she was appointed eight guards who stayed near her at all times.

There was a Eucharistic ceremony especially for young people, and Mother Teresa was asked at the last moment to give a talk at the end of the liturgy. She was told about a Youth Program called SIGN in which young people across the country and in some foreign countries concentrated on works of mercy for the sick, the needy and the lonely. Their motto was: "To help another in God's name is to give a sign of His kingdom and to proclaim Jesus' message of love."

Mother Teresa made the sign of the cross on her lips with her thumb. She asked the Holy Spirit to give her the words He wanted her to speak and she began: "Jesus said to the people of His time, 'If you want to be my disciples, take up your cross and follow me.'"

As with every crowd who listened to Mother Teresa, the young people were silent, holding on to every word, each one feeling as though Mother were speaking just for them, words that could change their life and give it new meaning.

Mother continued, "Today, in young people all over the world, Jesus lives His passion, in the suffering, in the hungry, the handicapped young people, in that child who eats a piece of bread crumb by crumb, because when that piece of bread is finished, there will be no more and hunger will come again. That is a station of the cross. Are you there with that child?

"And those thousands who die not only for bread, but for a little bit of love, of recognition. That is a station of the cross. Are you there?

"And young people, when they fall, as Jesus fell again and again for us, are we there as Simon Cyrene was, to pick them up, to pick up the cross?

"The people in the parks, the alcoholics, the homeless, they are looking at you. Do not be those who look and do not see. Look and see.

"We can begin the stations of the cross step by step with joy. Jesus made Himself the bread of life for us. We have Jesus in the bread of life to give us strength."

After her talk, the young people told Mother Teresa about their twenty-year-old friend and Co-Worker Eileen Potts who had just been diagnosed with leukemia and was at that moment in a hospital outside of Philadelphia. "Eileen is the leader of the SIGN movement. She's the one responsible for the large youth participation in the Congress, and after all her work she's too sick to attend."

Mother managed to slip away from the Congress to go to the hospital for a visit with Eileen. "I wanted to meet the young woman who worked so hard to make the Eucharistic Congress a success."

"Mother Teresa, is it really you?"

Mother laughed. "I hope so," she said.

"I was so looking forward to meeting you, Mother," Eileen said.

"I've been looking forward to meeting you too," Mother told her.

"Do you think I'm going to die, Mother?" Eileen asked her.

"We're all going to die when God calls us home. Some of us go young, some much older but we all go when it's our time to go."

"I guess you're right, Mother," Eileen said. "There were just so many things I wanted to do for Him on this earth before I go home."

"Just do whatever He asks you. Give Him whatever He asks for and take whatever He gives you and keep smiling at Him."

"I'll try, Mother," Eileen promised.

Two years later Eileen went home to God.

On August 5th, 1976, Dorothy Day, co-founder of the Catholic Worker Movement and the Hospitality Houses for the poor, spent the night in the same convent as Mother Teresa. They had first met in New York City in 1960 when Mother stopped there on her way home from Las Vegas.

The two old friends were delighted to see each other again. Besides their complete surrender of themselves to God and their decision to serve Him in the poor, the two women had something else in common, their great love for St. Thérèse of the Child Jesus, the Little Flower. Dorothy Day had published a book about her life and Mother Teresa has chosen her as her patron when she became a nun. And they both followed her little way of spiritual sanctity doing ordinary things with extraordinary love.

Dorothy Day spoke on August 6th at a general session entitled "Woman and the Eucharist." She said, "Our Creator gave us life and the Eucharist to sustain life. But we have given the world instruments of death of inconceivable magnitude." She was very disappointed that the organizers of the Congress had forgotten that August 6th was the anniversary of the bombing of Hiroshima. Instead of scheduling a penitential service on that day, they had planned a Mass for the military. "Women are born to nourish, not to destroy life," Dorothy said. She asked the women in the audience to do penance for the sins of war and destruction.

The women were still applauding Dorothy Day when Mother Teresa came to speak. Mother began her talk by saying, "Mary can truly say of Jesus, 'This is my body.' It was by surrendering herself that she became the mother of God. And when His followers deserted Jesus, it was Mary who stayed with Him. Do we remain with our people when they are disowned, thrown out, when they suffer? Do we give them our understanding love?"

As she ended her talk, Mother said, "It is the Bicentennial Year of the United States of America and I wish to give you a very special gift.

"I will give you a new foundation of the Missionaries of Charity," Mother told her audience, "the Contemplative Sisters who will live the Word of God in Eucharistic adoration and contemplation."

Several years earlier, Mother Teresa had been traveling through France with Father Georges Gorrée when she got an inspiration: "I would love to see each of my houses adopted by a contemplative community."

"If you're serious, Mother," Father Gorrée said, "I'll see that you have at least one contemplative convent praying for each of your active convents." By September 1975, after just one year, over 400 contemplative convents in Europe had enthusiastically accepted this spiritual adoption. Mother was so delighted with the situation, she decided to form her own contemplative order. When she and Sister Nirmala first talked of a contemplative branch, they spoke of putting it in the peaceful setting of the Himalayas.

But at the Eucharistic Congress, Mother received the inspiration that America was ready for a contemplative branch and what better gift to give the United States for her Bicentennial birthday?

Eileen Egan closed the meeting by saying, "The Eucharist can be seen as a foretaste of the heavenly banquet in which all people are reconciled to God and to one another.

"Dorothy Day and Mother Teresa are creating a theology of Peace in carrying out Jesus' commands to feed, clothe and shelter Him despite the attitudes or actions of societies and nations."

The meeting ended with nearly a million people, most of them women, standing in silent prayer in memory of those who died at Hiroshima and for all victims of violence in all wars and all military personnel who in good conscience carry out orders in warfare.

Eileen then took Mother to Walden Pond near Concord to see the little cabin where Henry Thoreau lived to meditate and write. As Mother and Eileen gazed at the pond through a wire fence, Eileen told Mother how Thoreau's essay "Civil Disobedience" had been a strong influence on Gandhi's thinking and actions.

"Thoreau seems to be one of your saints," Mother told her.

"He is one of my favorite people," Eileen said.

"I am glad to learn about a man who influenced Gandhi, the father of our country," Mother Teresa said.

Mother Teresa then visited her Sisters in the Bronx. Sister Nirmala, who had led the first team of Sisters to the New World, was made superior of the new branch which was modeled after earlier contemplative orders such as the Carmelites with prayer and meditation at the center of the Sisters' lives. Traditional contemplative Sisters never left their convent until their death, but the new contemplatives would be different in that they would not live inside the convent at all times, communicating only through a grill.

The Missionaries of Charity Contemplatives would leave their convent for Mass each morning and open their convent to anyone who wished to pray and meditate. Each day they would spend two hours visiting shut-ins or sick people in hospitals or talking to people in the street about God's love.

Mother Teresa told all of her Missionaries, Co-Workers and friends, "We must be contemplatives in the world. How can we last even one day without hearing Jesus say, 'I love you'? Impossible. Our soul needs that as much as the body needs to breathe the air. Contemplation is listening to Jesus. His message is always 'I love you.'"

On September 8th, to celebrate Our Lady's birthday, Sister Nirmala took all her Contemplative Sisters to Crotona Park in the South Bronx, not far from their convent. All of the Sisters were praying when a young man in a black suit began shouting, "What did Jeremiah say? He prophesied that God will work His anger. He will pour out His anger and blood will flow on the earth."

Sister Nirmala quoted the Prince of Peace giving His peace to all of humanity.

"I am preparing for war!" the man shouted. "I am an instrument of destruction." He held up two fingers as a sign of victory.

"What is your name?" Sister Nirmala asked.

"My name is Hassan."

"Hassan means good," Sister Nirmala said. "You can't be an instrument of destruction with that name."

Hassan walked up to Sister Nirmala and pulled out a switchblade. He pointed the knife at her throat. Automatically, she lifted up her cross, holding it up with the Rosary. "These are my only weapons," she said. "They mean love. They mean that the lion and the lamb can live together in peace." The other Sisters came and gathered around. He withdrew his knife and joined the Sisters in their prayers and hymns. When he was leaving, he promised, "I will protect you in this park as if I am the guardian angel of the place!" They would see him many times after that and each time he was subdued when he greeted them.

When she left the Bronx, Mother went to Rome for a retreat with her Sisters there, and then she went to the second international Co-Workers' meeting in Lippstadt, Germany.

Then she went to France to the little town of Taizé where she visited the Ecumenical Center run by Brother Roger Schutz, a Protestant, who had been blessed by Pope John XXIII in his efforts to reconcile all Christians. Mother Teresa joined Brother Roger for evening prayers in the parish church. Over 3,000 young people crowded into the chapel. Together they prayed for unity and peace. Both Mother Teresa and Brother Roger were saddened by the divisions among Christians and both prayed constantly for unity. They asked God to bless all humanity with love of God and love of one another.

On November 25, 1976, Mother Teresa spoke at the World Conference on Religion and Peace in Singapore. "We do not need guns and bombs," she said. "We need love and compassion to overcome evil . . . All the works of love are works of peace."

For the next three years, Mother Teresa traveled the earth answering calls for help from locations where few Sisters lived or where huge populations lived in poverty or where natural disasters took lives and homes from many people.

In 1976 she opened centers in six new countries outside of India. In 1977 she opened seven and in 1978 there were twenty-five new foundations of the Missionaries of Charity, sixteen of them in India. By the end of 1979, there would be 158 foundations.

On June 8, 1978, Mother opened her first house in Yugoslavia, at Zagreb, Sister Mary Magdalene's hometown, where Mother Teresa had said her last good-bye to her mother and sister before going to Ireland and eventually to India.

When an Albanian priest spoke to Mother Teresa, she told him, "I can't speak the language anymore, Father. I haven't practiced it for fifty years."

He told her, "Mother Teresa, you speak the language of the soul which everyone everywhere understands."

She looked at him very seriously and said, "You are right, Father. That language alone can bring us all together."

On June 10th, Sunday, there was a solemn Mass celebrated by Msgr. Michael Cecchini, the Apostolic Nuncio in Belgrade, with Archbishop Kuharic, his vicar, Bishop Skvore, and many other priests and deacons. The Archbishop introduced Mother Teresa, an Albanian, to her people. He also introduced the four Sisters who would be living in Zagreb, one of them was also an Albanian, Sister Martha Kerhanaj from Zjum, the first Albanian to join the Missionaries of Charity.

When Mother spoke, she said, "When my mother finally consented to my entry into the convent, she told me, 'All right, my child, go; but always remain God's servant and Christ's.' If I am not faithful to my vocation, I shall be judged by my mother, not by God. Someday she is going to ask me, 'My daughter, have you lived for God alone?'"

The Archbishop of Zagreb told Mother Teresa that he was a Co-Worker and that the Co-Worker movement had spread throughout Yugoslavia.

When they left Zagreb, Mother Teresa and her friend Father Michael Gabric, another Co-Worker priest, visited Skopje, Mother's birthplace. "I want to visit my father's grave," Mother Teresa said. They went to the graveyard, but in 1963 an earthquake had destroyed the cemetery where her father was buried. Mother Teresa stood looking at the remains of the cemetery and said, "I don't know where my mother or my sister are buried. I thought I could find my father's grave." She sighed. "It doesn't matter. They are all together now. They are happy with Jesus and His mother." She fell to her knees where she was and spent time in silent prayer.

Her childhood home and the little Sacred Heart Church where she had made her first communion and where she'd gone looking for a priest to give her father the Last Rites were both gone also, destroyed in the quake.

She felt a great desire to make a pilgrimage to Our Lady of Letnice, a shrine a short distance from Skopje. Father Michael went with her. "It was at Letnice that I first heard God's voice," she said. "My vocation convinced me that I should serve God and be at His disposal. I remember the feast of Mary's Assumption. I was in front of Mary's altar with a burning candle in my hand, singing with my heart ready to burst. I decided, 'I want to belong only to God!' And I asked Our Lady to keep me faithful to Him always." With great joy and deep devotion, she knelt before the statue. After a long period of prayer, she got up and looked into Our Lady's face. "They changed her dress," she said. "It is not the one she wore long ago. But her eyes and her face are still the same. Blessed Mother, please help me return to Skopje with some Sisters to open a house in my hometown."

In 1979, Mother went with Sister Damina to war-ravaged Beirut, Lebanon to look for a house. They found themselves on a street where two groups were shooting at each other from opposite sides. They wanted to shout, "Stop shooting!" in Arabic, but they were so frightened they forgot the words. Finally Mother shouted in English, "Stop!" The firing stopped and the two nuns continued to walk down the center of the road. They would find just the house they wanted. When they returned to Beirut to begin work, Mother took her nuns and filled the house with victims of the conflict, orphans, and all those in need of help.

Mother Teresa tried to attend all Missionaries of Charity openings. Her Indian passport allowed her to enter every country since India was unaligned in the Cold War. In addition, the Holy Father had given her a diplomatic passport from the Vatican. Whenever Mother could not be present at an opening, she sent her Sisters with a request to the church and the Co-Workers: "Please protect the poverty of my Sisters. Their poverty is their dowry." Several times overly helpful Co-Workers prepared homes for the Sisters with luxurious carpets, comfortable furniture and washers and dryers. The Sisters immediately pulled up the carpets and gave the "excess" furniture, washers and dryers to the poor. More than one convent had a long line of poor people outside who heard the Sisters were giving away brand new washers and dryers. Someone told Mother Teresa, "Mother, you are spoiling the poor." Mother laughed and said, "If you realized what the poor go through, you would know they deserve spoiling." Then, getting serious, she said, "And Jesus lives in the poorest of the poor. He tells us so Himself. It isn't possible to spoil Jesus."

The Nobel Prize

On October 16, 1979, Mother Teresa went to Nirmal Hriday, the Home for the Dying, near the temple of Kali, just as she did every day when she was in Calcutta. A man was brought in covered with maggots. Mother sat down next to him and began to clean him efficiently, speaking to him gently in Bengali.

"I am thirsty," the man mumbled. Mother Teresa went for a glass of water. He drank the water, smiled, said a weak "Thank you," and then he died.

"He went home with a smile," Mother said.

At 5:30 that afternoon, Mother Teresa returned home for the evening adoration of the Blessed Sacrament in the chapel. She was upset to find dozens of reporters, photographers and film-makers crowded around the Mother House. Some of them had even managed to get inside, although this was strictly against regulations. Ignoring the reporters, Mother went straight to Sister Mary Agnes. "What are these people doing here, Sister?" she asked.

"Why, you've won the Nobel Peace Prize, Mother, and they've come to speak with you."

Mother gasped, took a deep breath, and said, "Please tell them to wait outside, Sister." Then she slipped quietly into the chapel.

Many people assume that winning the Nobel Peace Prize was the crowning achievement of Mother Teresa's life. It is perhaps difficult to realize that from her point of view it was a tragedy. As she knelt in the simple chapel, Mother identified with Jesus in the Garden of Gethsemane when He prayed, "Father, if it is possible, let this cup pass from me; yet not as I will, but as You will."

All her life she had envied contemplative nuns who spent their days in prayer and sacrifice behind convent walls. Mother Teresa thought of St. Thérèse of Lisieux, who never left her convent from the day she entered. And yet, the Little Flower had dreamed all her brief life of being a missionary in the field and offered her prayers and sacrifices each day for the priests and religious in the missions. After her death, when the Church officially declared St. Thérèse a saint, they made her co-patron of those missions she had longed to visit.

Mother said, "Jesus, what in the world are You up to now, having me win this prize?"

In her head, Mother could hear the other Teresa, St.Teresa of Avila, saying to God, "If this is how You treat your friends, it's no wonder You have so few of them!"

She smiled at the private joke between the three Teresas and God. "When I was a little girl reading books about saints," she said to God, "I used to pray to You, 'Lord, make me a martyr.' What I meant was for You to allow me to die for love of You. I was not praying for a life where I would be miserable." She caught herself and laughed aloud. The other Sisters had entered the chapel one by one. They looked up at the sound of her laughter and breathed a sigh of relief. They had a great feeling of joy and gratitude that the work was being appreciated and the world was coming to know the poorest of the poor. But they also recognized the great strain and suffering this would put on their beloved Mother Teresa. She no longer belonged just to them and the poor. Now the whole world would claim her.

"I don't deserve the prize," Mother thought. "But it is not for me. It's for the poor that I will receive the prize." Her heart then filled with joy. The world was coming to see and love the poor. "Thank you, Lord, for Your gift to the poorest of the poor." She continued her private conversation with God. "You are right, Lord. You know what kind of martyrdom You need from each of us. When You asked the rich young man to sell all he had, give it to the poor and follow You, it was the hardest thing in the world for him to do. But that was not why You asked it of him. It was the thing he needed to do for his own salvation. He had to free himself of his attachments so he could cling to You."

The Sisters then entered the chapel and after awhile began singing a hymn of thanksgiving. Mother joined them.

Crowds gathered around the Mother House. People from all walks of life began to knock on the door. They all came to tell Mother Teresa how happy they were. Photographers and journalists begged for interviews and pictures.

Mother asked the Nobel Prize Committee, "How much money do you usually spend on the reception dinner?"

"Around $6,000."

"Wonderful!" Mother said. "That will feed 400 of our people for a whole year. Could you please cancel the dinner and give me the money?"

"Well, Mother Teresa, that has never been done before, but I'll see what we can do."

"Thank you. God bless you."

The Committee sent Mother Teresa three tickets to Oslo, one for herself, and one each for Sister Mary Agnes and Sister Mary Gertrude. The Sisters wondered what kind of reception Mother would have since the banquet held at the Hotel Continental had always been a gala affair, one of the highlights of the award ceremony festivals. They wondered if people would be disappointed.

During the long flight, Mother prayed her Rosary, read a spiritual book and ate a slice of bread with lettuce and tomato. She made a few notes for her acceptance speech. In some ways, this would be the most important speech she had ever made. The idea of speaking to so many people make her feel weak. "Lord, I offer it all up to You. I know You will use me to bring more souls to You."

When they landed in Oslo, it was late afternoon. The sun had already set, and the cold November air was only 14°F. Carrying all her worldly goods in her home-made cloth bag, Mother stepped out of the plane. She wore her regular inexpensive sari, with sandals and a man's navy blue sweater. The Sisters had been offered coats and fur boots but, characteristically, they turned them down. Mother Teresa was surprised to see a long line of people holding candles. They had braved the cold night to welcome her and show their love and respect. No other recipient in the history of the Nobel Prize had ever received such a warm welcome.

Her trip to Oslo was a festive occasion for many people, but for her it was a time of great suffering. "Mother, how do you feel about winning the Nobel Peace Prize?" a reporter asked her.

"It is a drop of deliverance in an ocean of suffering," Mother said. "I am myself unworthy of the prize. I do not want it personally. But by this award the Norwegian people have recognized the existence of the poor. It is on their behalf that I have come."

Meanwhile, when word of the award reached Bengal, its chief minister Jyoti Basu, a Communist, held a reception in honor of Mother Teresa. "You have long been the mother of Bengal," he said. "Now you are the mother of the world."

India's President Giri added, "Mother Teresa is among those emancipated souls who have transcended all barriers of race, religion, creed, and nation."

In Oslo, a thanksgiving ceremony was held in the Lutheran Cathedral. Afterwards a thousand people carrying lighted candles walked through the streets with Mother Teresa leading the procession. It was a clear, starry night with bitter cold air.

They went to a mission hall in Oslo where some girls gave Mother Teresa a check for about $300. "This money was all donated by children out of their pocket money," she told Mother. Young people all over Norway had collected money. Together they raised over $70,000. Mother put her hands together and solemnly bowed to them in the Indian way of expressing gratitude.

"Yes, money is necessary," she told the children, "but we must take care to increase its value by seasoning it with love."

On December 10th, the King of Norway welcomed his international guests who had gathered in a palace at the University of Oslo for the Nobel Prize ceremony. From Skopje, the town where Mother Teresa was born, had come Nikola Prela, the

Catholic Bishop. From Palermo, Italy had come her brother Lazar Bojaxhiu and his daughter. Jacqueline de Decker had come from Belgium, wearing steel braces that allowed her to move. Ann Blaikie had come from England. There were Co-Workers from Sweden, Denmark, Finland, Holland, France, Switzerland, Italy, Malta, and the United States.

The President of the Nobel Committee, Mr. John Sannes, said, quoting an Indian journalist, "The Sisters, with their serene ways, their saris, their knowledge of local languages . . . have come to symbolize not only the best in Christian charity, but also the best in Indian culture and civilization from Buddha to Ghandhi." He added, "Mother Teresa works in the world as she finds it, in the slums of Calcutta and other towns and cities. But she makes no distinction between poor and rich persons, between poor and rich countries. Politics has never been her concern, but economic, social, and political work with these same aims are in complete harmony with her own life's work."

He ended his speech saying, "Mother Teresa deserves Nobel's Peace Prize because she promotes peace in the most fundamental manner, by her confirmation of the inviolability of human dignity."

The huge crowded hall was silent as the tiny Catholic nun walked up to the speaker's stand. She bowed to the immense audience in her traditional Indian style. On behalf of the Nobel Prize Committee, President Sannes placed the gold medal and the gift of $190,000 in her hand. Mother thanked him and smiled. She waited until he was in his seat, then she began to talk without the assistance of notes.

"Let us all thank God on this beautiful occasion, for the joy of spreading peace, the joy of loving one another and the joy of recognizing that the poorest of the poor are our brothers and sisters.

"Let us thank God for the opportunity that we all have today, for this gift of peace that reminds us that we have been created to live that peace, and Jesus became man to bring that Good News to the poor."

She spoke from her heart about things that mattered deeply to her. Once she began to talk about the poorest of the poor, the dying, the abandoned babies, she completely forgot her own fears and discomfort and felt grateful to God for having the chance to speak about Him in the least of His people.

While she spoke, everyone in the great hall was silent. The large room was overflowing with hundreds of people outside in the corridors. Every one of them was spellbound by what Mother was saying and the spirit with which she said it.

Of abortion, she said, "We are teaching our beggars, our leprosy patients, our slum dwellers, our people of the street, natural family planning. And in Calcutta alone in six years—it is all in Calcutta—we have had 61,273 babies less from the families who would have had them because they practice this natural way of abstaining, of self-control, out of love for each other. And our poor people understand. And you know what they have told me? 'Our family is healthy, our family is united, and we can have a baby whenever we want.'" She went on to say that if the beggars on the street could make such strides, how much the world stands to learn from their lesson.

Mother Teresa told them about the poorest of the poor in Calcutta, the people dying in the streets, the lepers and the abandoned babies. "The poor people are great people," she said. "They can teach us so many beautiful things."

She ended her speech by saying, ". . . we must live life beautifully, we have Jesus with us and He loves us. If we could only remember that God loves us, and we have an opportunity to love others as He loves us, not in big things, but in small things with great love, then Norway becomes a nest of love. And how beautiful it will be that from here a center for peace from war has been given. That from here the joy of life of the unborn child comes out. If you become a burning light of peace in the world, then really the Nobel Peace Prize is a gift of the Norwegian people. God bless you!"

Mother announced she would give the prize money and the banquet money to feed the poor and to build more homes for the homeless and the lepers.

After she finished speaking, some Swedish feminists who admired Mother's work with the poor asked her, "But what about the rights of the pregnant woman, Mother? Aren't you concerned with her rights?"

"I care greatly for every human being from their conception to their last breath. God loves all of us. Jesus said whatever we do to the least of His people, we do to Him. Who could be less than the little unborn baby whose scream is silence? We must love God's children everywhere. That is all He asks of us."

After the award ceremony, there was a simple reception where the Nobel Prize Committee and Mother Teresa greeted the guests in person. Mother Teresa did not eat anything at all at the reception, drinking only a glass of water, since Mother's order would not eat or drink anywhere except in the convent so as not to embarrass poor people who had nothing.

During the reception, one of the Co-Workers asked, "Mother Teresa, could we see your gold medal?" "Of course," Mother said. She began looking, but she couldn't remember where she had put it. So there was a frantic search for it. Mother remained cool, saying her Rosary while they searched. A Co-Worker found the medal between the stack of winter coats on a shelf near the entrance to the hall.

Mother stood up to greet each person who approached her and gave them her "God bless you" response.

It was not the crowds she dreaded, not even when they rushed towards her, surrounding her, trying to touch the hem of her garments. They saw Christ in her just as she saw Him in them. What she disliked was all the praise showered on her. Mother told her Co-Workers, "Some Americans said, 'Mother, they want to canonize you.' And I told them, 'Let me die first.'"

Before she left Oslo, Mother Teresa received a long-distance phone call from Mrs. Violet Collins, National Link for the Co-Workers in the United States. "Mother, there is a burning issue in the United States right now. American Embassy personnel in Teheran are being held captive. Some of their families are meeting in Washington D.C. and they wanted to know if you would personally intercede on their behalf and ask for their freedom."

"I will visit the Embassy of Iran as soon as I get to Rome," Mother Teresa promised.

Saying good-bye to her Co-Workers, Mother told them, "To be able to pray for peace we must first of all be able to listen. For God speaks in the silence of the heart and that is the beginning of peace. Let us radiate the peace of God and so light His light and extinguish in the world and in every heart all hatred and love of power.

"Let us in every country, wherever we are, meet God with a smile. Everywhere and in everyone. A smile is the beginning of world peace."

When she was leaving Oslo, Mother told Sister Agnes and Sister Gertrude, "Hopefully this will be the last award ceremony I shall be called to attend. We can use the prize money for our lepers and our poor, but all these appearances are interferring with our work."

Raising Consciousness

When she arrived in Rome, Mother Teresa went to the Embassy of Iran. It was December 13, 1979, and all of America was concerned with the fate of the hostages, who'd been taken when the American Embassy in Iran was seized by Islamic Revolutionaries led by Ayatollah Khomieni.

The staff member who opened the door asked, "What can I do for you?"

"I have been asked to see you about the American hostages," Mother Teresa said. "I know nothing. I have been too busy to read anything. I come to you as a mother who longed for her children. People have appealed to me to do this. I am willing to go to Iran or to talk to the Ayatollah on the telephone."

"I will look into the matter for you," the man said.

Mother replied, "Meantime, we will be praying."

Mother and her Sisters kept praying about the hostages, but there was no response from the Embassy of Iran; Mother wasn't even given a chance to talk to the authorities on the telephone. (There were rumors later on that the Iranians were ready to release the hostages at this point but certain American politicians wanted them to wait until after the American Presidential election.)

While she was in Rome, Mother attended a Mass celebrated by Pope John Paul II in his private chapel. Mother Teresa presented her proposal for a new Co-Worker organization made up of priests. He asked, "May I be the first priest to volunteer, Mother?"

For the first time, she was able to go into the Catacombs, the underground galley with side recesses for tombs where the early Christians hid from Roman soldiers and where great saints like St. Agnes, St. Sebastian and St. Celia were buried.

She returned to India, and learned that her adopted country was preparing to honor her with its highest civilian award, the Bharat Ratna, the Jewel of India. The ceremony took place in the presidential palace in Delhi. This was the first time ever the award was being given to a naturalized Indian.

Walking to the sounds of the Indian national anthem, Mother Teresa approached President Neelam Sanjiva Reddy, who said, "She embodies in herself compassion and love of humanity as few in history have done." Mother accepted the award from the President with one of her beautiful smiles. Prime Minister Indira Gandhi came forward to congratulate her. Later on Mrs. Gandhi said, "To meet her is to feel utterly humble, to sense the power of tenderness and the strength of love."

Mother Teresa was raising the consciousness of the entire world, helping people realize that works of mercy, feeding the hungry, giving shelter to the homeless, caring for the ill, clothing the naked are truly works of peace—indeed the very foundation of a peaceful world.

Everywhere she went, people asked Mother Teresa for her autograph. She would write, "God bless you. M. Teresa M.C."

One of the Sisters asked her, "Don't you get tired of writing your signature, Mother?"

"For me, it is like praying," Mother said. "When I write 'God bless you' I am praying for the person. It is something I do for the people. They appreciate it."

The Holy Father gave Mother Teresa the keys to the Primaville building, a beautiful mansion on Vatican property. "Now you will have a place where every single child, every homeless mother awaiting a child can always be welcome."

"Thank you, Your Holiness," Mother said. "Abortion is nothing but fear of the child, fear to have to feed one more child, to have to educate one more child, to have to love one more child. Therefore the child must die. If there is no one who wants the child, I want it."

In 1980, Mother took a team of Sisters to settle in Skopje, Yugoslavia, her birthplace. Her prayer to Our Lady of Letnice was answered.

When Mother was in Australia to start another house, she agreed to be on a radio program run by Reverend Fred Niles, a well-known Protestant minister. A caller told Mother Teresa, "I am nervous. This is my first time on a call-in program." Mother Teresa said, "Me too."

In May 1981, Mother celebrated the fiftieth anniversary of her life as a nun. There was a Mass at the Mother House in Calcutta with a bishop and many priests. In June 1981, she was in New York where Cardinal Cooke was the main celebrant at another Thanksgiving Mass for her anniversary.

"These fifty years have been fifty years of love," she told the people at the Mass. "Let us thank God together for what He has done. Not only through me, but through the whole society, for the lepers, the dying and the unwanted. We are all the body of Christ. Our faith in Him must prove itself in works. Today, I thank the Archdiocese for inviting me here, and I thank all of you for accepting us to work with you."

On June 4, 1981, President and Mrs. Ronald Reagan invited Mother Teresa to lunch at the White House. She took Sister Priscilla and Mrs. Violet Collins, National Co-Worker Link.

Mother told the President, referring to his having been shot by a madman earlier that year, "Your suffering after the attempt on your life has brought you closer to Jesus and to the poor who suffer so much."

Afterward, when reporters asked him what he told Mother Teresa, President Reagan said, "I listened."

Mother Teresa sent the President one of her little cards to thank him for his hospitality. The card read: "The presence of nuclear arms in the world has created fear and distrust among nations, as it is one more weapon to destroy human life—God's beautiful presence in the world. Just as abortion is used to kill the unborn child, this new weapon will become a means to eliminate the Poor of the World, our Brothers and Sisters whom Jesus has taught us to love, as He has loved each one of us. God bless you. M. Teresa M.C."

When Mother Teresa was awarded the Discovery Medal later that month at Marquette University in Milwaukee, Wisconsin, reporters asked her, "Have you made any discoveries, Mother?"

"I am too small to discover anything," she said. Then she added, "Yes, I suppose it is a discovery for some that the poorest of the poor, the rejected, the throwaways among us . . . they are Jesus in His disguise."

Mother Teresa had passed her seventieth birthday and someone asked, "Have you decided when you are going to retire, Mother?" It appeared she had never thought of retirement. She was quiet for a few seconds. Then she said, "The poor cannot retire."

Mother Teresa's brother Lazar died of lung cancer at his home in Italy July 3rd. When Mother got the news, she went into the chapel where she said her Rosary and sat in silence. When she returned, she said, "My mother must be rejoicing now. She must have been longing for him to join her, Papa and Aga. Now she's with her only son whom she loved more than her life. He died a beautiful death. It was really going home to God. Now it only remains for Our Father to call me and the whole family will be united once more. It's all in His hands. He knows what He's doing."

Some people criticized Mother Teresa for not trying to change the structures of society. A reporter discussing the Habitat Forum in Vancouver, Canada, felt that Mother Teresa was out of place there because she made it too easy to dump one's guilt about poverty and homelessness by a donation without confronting the reality of the problem. Mother often refused gifts saying she wanted action, not money. She wanted people to work with the poor, to learn to love and respect them to see

Jesus in them and in themselves.

In 1985, for example, when the one of the Missionaries of Charity homes was overcrowded with novices, a rich landowner offered Mother a house on the same street. Mother said, "I don't want your housc, I want you. Come work with us."

Mother always said, "Giving need not be confined to money or material goods. I would like more people to give their hands to serve and their hearts to love, to recognize the poor in their own homes, towns and countries and to reach out to them in love and compassion."

In many interviews she explained, "We give fish to the poor instead of giving them a fishing rod because our people are too weak from hunger, too diseased and disabled, too old or too young to fish for themselves. What I do, I give them fish to eat and when they are strong enough, we'll hand them over to you and you give them the rod and show them how to catch the fish."

Mother was criticized for many things. Some people felt she should not have run homes for the sick and dying if she didn't have the modern medical methods. Perhaps they failed to realize that Mother cared for people who were too poor or too sick to be cared for in traditional medical settings. Many people would rather have died surrounded by Mother Teresa's loving nuns than in a sterile hospital attached to all sorts of life-support machines.

She was criticized for socializing and accepting help from people like the widow of Enver Hoxha, Communist dictator of Albania (who would not allow her mother and sister to leave the country), Baby Doc Duvalier, the ruthless dictator of Haiti, and several questionable businessmen including Charles Keating.

Journalist and author Christopher Hitchens, a very vocal critic of Mother Teresa, accused her of spending millions of dollars on convents rather than building new hospitals. It's safe to say that anyone who was ever inside one of Mother's convents would conclude that less money was spent on them than on most of the poor huts, shacks and houses around them.

In El Florido, Mexico, Mother Teresa refused new washing machines and dryers for her orphanage which had been given to her. She gave them to the poor who had come for help which left the Sisters to wash all the babies clothes and diapers by hand with a wash board and hard soap.

Mother was prepared to shake hands with a convicted murderer, a leper, or someone who saw themselves as her enemy. To her, everyone was Christ in His various masks. If one understands Mother's theology, it can be seen why she did this. She lived for love and forgave everyone. She followed the Bible literally. "Love your God with all your heart, all your strength, all your soul and love your neighbor as yourself." Mother didn't see borders and frontiers. She saw the world as one and she loved us all. "Judge not, lest you be judged," she said.

When Mother Teresa visited the town of St. Paul in the province of Alberta, Canada, Bishop Raymond Roy presented her with a gift of $925,000. All of the money had been raised by the residents of this tiny town. They explained how it came about. "A group of us attended the Habitat Conference in Vancouver in 1976, Mother Teresa. Your talk inspired us and we returned home determined to help the lepers, the lonely and the lost. We called our group the Habitat Institute and with partially donated labor and construction materials we built a house. We counted on selling the house for $50,000 but it sold several times and each time the buyer made a large donation, so we ended up with almost a million dollars for your work, Mother."

In 1982, she was presented with an honorary Doctorate of Law by Harvard University and received two standing ovations from the audience, in spite of the fact that many of them disagreed with her ideas on chastity, abortion and birth control. In her audience was a group of children who had been adopted by Boston families from Shishu Bhavan, the children's home in Calcutta.

When a Co-Worker said, "Congratulations, Mother Teresa, now you have a doctorate from Harvard," Mother replied, "I do not know why Jesus does things like this." She shrugged her shoulders and continued, "It seems Jesus is using me as an instrument to bring people together to talk about God. That is really wonderful, a new hope for the world."

When Mother Teresa visited Jenkins, Kentucky in 1982, the local newspapers carried stories about the Catholic nun who had won the Nobel Peace Prize and was now visiting Kentucky. When Mother decided to take her Sisters into the little village in eastern Kentucky, she knew she was taking them into a setting like none they had lived in before. Mother and Sister Priscilla had visited the "hollows," the hills and valleys of Appalachia, before deciding upon this tiny mining town. They respected the proud nature of these hardworking mountain people.

Catholics made up less than one percent of the area's population and many of them had never seen a Catholic nun before. But they accepted the Missionaries of Charity with courtesy and hospitality, offering a coffee and pie. The Sisters thanked them with a gentle no, not bothering to explain the rule that they're not to eat anything away from the convent.

A lighted sign placed on the main street read: "Welcome, Mother Teresa." Hundreds of local people attended the outdoor prayer service. Mother Teresa was presented with a gift, a statue of the Virgin Mary carved out of coal. "Thank you so much," Mother said. "Never have I possessed such a rare statue of Our Lady."

When the people of Jenkins read in the newspapers that Mother Teresa had won her Nobel Peace Prize for working with the poorest of the poor, however, some of them got upset. "We ain't got no poorest of the poor around here," they insisted proudly.

"Then we'll just have to help anyone who could do with some help," one of the Sisters told them. The people thought about this and accepted the offer.

For two years in a row, 1981 and 1982, polls showed Mother Teresa was the most admired woman in the world.

Someone sent Mother Teresa a copy of the *London Times* near the end of 1982. It included a photograph of an elderly man on his knees receiving the Eucharist directly in his mouth from the hands of a priest.

"Thank you, Jesus," Mother said. The man in the picture was Malcolm Muggeridge, the writer whose book *Something Beautiful for God* had introduced many people to Mother's work. Mother Teresa had been praying for Malcolm to know Jesus in the Eucharist ever since they attended Mass together more than a decade earlier. She remembered how Malcolm had told her, "The various controversies and conflicts now shaking the church make it impossible for me to accept your way of looking at the church's present predicament."

She had told him, "Jesus hand-picked twelve apostles. One of them proved to be a crook and the others ran away. Why, then, should we expect the Popes to do better?" Mother Teresa had explained to Malcolm how much the Eucharist meant to her. "I could not get through one single day or hour of the life He has chosen for me without Jesus in the Eucharist." She had a difficult time understanding Malcolm's hesitation from full participation in the Mass since she noticed his great devotion during the liturgy. Now, years later, Malcolm and his wife had come to know Jesus in the Blessed Sacrament. Mother Teresa rejoiced.

Never Saying No

In June of 1982, the fragile peace between Lebanon and Israel was shattered when Israel charged that the PLO (Palestine Liberation Organization) had critically wounded the Israeli ambassador in London. Israel attacked southern Lebanon, demolishing PLO strongholds. On June 10th Israeli troops reached Beirut and forced the PLO guerrillas from the western sector and practically destroyed it.

Pope John Paul II received Mother Teresa at his summer residence in the hills outside of Rome. "I really wanted to go to Lebanon myself," the Holy Father said, "but the Cardinals felt it was impossible to arrange the appropriate security. Then I heard that you were planning to go."

"Yes, Your Holiness, I am concerned about my Sisters who are working there and I have heard about some abandoned children."

"Mother Teresa, I would like you to be my personal envoy to Lebanon where that terrible war is being waged."

They knelt together in the Pope's private chapel and prayed for peace in Lebanon and for a refuge for the homeless Palestinians.

She said, "Bless me, Holy Father. Pray for me that I won't ruin God's work."

"Pray for me that I won't ruin His church," responded Pope John Paul II.

Mother Teresa took a plane from Rome to Athens, then another plane to Cyprus. From Cyprus, the only means of reaching Beirut was a seventeen hour boat ride. She found her Sisters safe in their convent in East Beirut. With Mother Teresa was a young American film-maker and Co-Worker, Ann Petrie, who had made a film about the Missionaries of Charity called "The World of Mother Teresa." When they arrived, they found bombing and shelling everywhere. The convent was within five miles of a major target. The area was full of snipers.

John de Salis, head of the Red Cross in Lebanon, told Mother Teresa, "There are some mentally ill children on the upper floor of a nursing home located near a camp of Palestinian refugees. The building has been bombed repeatedly. All of the caretakers have been killed or have run away. Those children don't have food or water and some of them may be wounded."

"All of the children can be housed with the Sisters at the refuge," Mother told him immediately.

"The main problem, Mother," continued Mr. de Salis, "is that the building is on the other side of the Green Line and no one can cross that line."

"We have to evacuate those children," Mother said. "I will cross the line."

The guards at the Green Line check-point explained to her, "You cannot go in there, Mother Teresa. There is a war going on. We can't allow you to go inside."

"What if there is a cease-fire?" Mother Teresa asked.

"Listen to those bombs, Mother. Does that sound like they are preparing for a cease-fire?"

"We have been praying for a cease-fire," Mother Teresa said. "And tomorrow is a feast day of the Blessed Mother. We have asked her to give us a cease-fire to celebrate her day."

"Aren't you asking a lot of the Blessed Mother?" the soldier said.

"Yes, but she always gives us a lot. She will give us the cease-fire."

"Listen, Mother Teresa," the soldier said. "If you get your cease-fire tomorrow, I will let you pass and I will even go with you to get the children."

"Thank you very much," Mother said with a big smile. "I will meet you here early tomorrow morning."

The next morning, there was indeed "a cease-fire of sorts." Although everyone else was against the project, Mother Teresa convinced Mr. de Salis to send four Red Cross vehicles into West Beirut to rescue the children. She traveled in the first one. When they were crossing the check-point, the guard asked, "Are you carrying any weapons?"

"Oh, yes," Mother Teresa said, "My prayer books and my Rosary." She held them up.

They found 38 children from ages 7 to 21, all completely helpless. They had no idea of what was going on about them. But they knew too well that they had no food or water and no care, and that they all felt weak, uncomfortable and afraid. Mother Teresa mingled with all the children, shaking hands with the older children and patting the younger ones. One by one, Mother Teresa, the International Red Cross workers, and the hospital workers picked up the children and carried or led them to the vehicles. They crossed the Green Line at an Israeli-controlled check-point and rushed the children to the Missionaries of Charity convent. Within a few minutes, the children were all cleaned, comforted and fed.

People who had lost much of their own possessions and supplies brought clothes, food, medical and cleaning supplies for the children. People found beds for the homeless children. Mother Teresa realized that in wartime most of the humanitarian efforts are concentrated on casualties. But the blind, the deaf, the insane, the elderly, and the babies need help and attention more than ever. Their needs are often overlooked during a war.

Two days later, Mother Teresa crossed the Green Line again to evacuate another 27 children.

One of the Red Cross workers said, "What surprised everyone was her energy. She saw the problem, fell to her knees, prayed for a few seconds, and then rattled off a list of supplies she needed. We didn't expect a saint to be so efficient."

The reporters who interviewed Mother Teresa in Beirut tried to get some political statements from her. Instead she read them St. Francis' beautiful prayer, "Lord, Make Me an Instrument of Your Peace." People who knew the life of St. Francis of Assisi knew that it was not far from Beirut where he had come personally with his message of peace to Crusaders committed to war.

Mother told the reporters, "I have never been in a war before, but I have seen famine and death. I was asking myself what they feel when they do this. I don't understand it. They are all children of God. Why do they do this? Let us not use bombs and guns to overcome the world," Mother said. "Let's use love and compassion."

When some of the soldiers tried to explain their ideas about defense, Mother said, "Today nations put too much effort and money into defending their borders. If they could only defend defenseless people with food, shelter and clothing, I think the world would be a happier place."

In wartime, when each side dehumanizes its enemy, Mother Teresa could be the conscience of both sides with her ability to point out the fact that our enemy is Jesus in His most distressing disguise.

"If everyone could see God in his neighbor, would we still need tanks and generals?" she asked.

August 6th was the feast of the Transfiguration of Jesus before His apostles Peter, James and John. They had climbed to the top of a mountain and the apostles saw Jesus in His divine nature surrounded by a white light, talking with Moses and Elijah. Mother Teresa reminded her Sisters that this same date was the anniversary of the destruction at Hiroshima. "This is the difference between the light that purifies and the light that destroys," she told them.

She wrote her friend Eileen Egan, "If you only knew how I long to light the fire of love and peace throughout the world. Pray for me that He may use me to the fullest."

On May 27, 1983, Mother Teresa met with the leaders of Caritas Internationalis at their general assembly in Rome. She spoke to the representatives of Catholic social services from all over the world. She told them, "You are carriers of God's love and people must be able to know your love for them. Not only words! Today more people are talking to the poor."

On May 30th, Pope John Paul II told Mother, "Mother Teresa, you look unusually tired. Please do me a favor and go for a medical checkup."

"There isn't time, Your Holiness," Mother said. "I'm fine."

On June 2nd she was hospitalized in Salvator Mundi Hospital after falling out of bed in the convent at San Gregorio in Rome. Once the doctors examined her, they sent for Sister Nirmala, Superior of the Contemplative Sisters in New York. They told Sister Nirmala, "Mother Teresa is on the verge of a major heart attack."

Mother was not even allowed to move her arms. She had to be fed all of her meals. At first her only visitors were Sister Nirmala and Sister Stella, the Superior of the Missionaries of Charity Sisters in Rome. When her doctor prescribed pain-killers, Mother refused to take them saying, "I want to offer up my sufferings to God." She did take the medicine for her poor blood circulation because she wanted to get well as soon as possible so she could go to her poor. The news of her hospitalization was carried around the world by the media. Every news program and every newspaper gave daily reports on the state of her health.

For a while it looked as if she were going to die. The world media focused on Mother Teresa the way India's media used to focus on Mahatma Gandhi during his long fasts in protest of British rule. People all over the world prayed for Mother's recovery. She received get-well cards, letters, and telegrams from everywhere.

A Hindu man in Kashmir wrote, "I am praying that Kali will take the bad part from your heart and give it to me and take the healthy part from me and give it to you."

The President of Yemen sent a cable, as did President Singh of India. President Reagan and his wife Nancy sent roses and wishes for a speedy recovery. Jyoti Basu, the Communist head of Bengal, wrote and the King and Queen of Belgium came to the hospital.

People offered to pay all her medical bills, but the doctors at Salvator Mundi would not take anything.

"It was such a beautiful gift to share in the passion of Christ," Mother said.

A priest brought the Eucharist every day from 9:00 a.m. to 10:00 a.m. for Adoration and each day he said a Mass in her room.

The doctors told Mother, "If you obey instructions and take your medicine you can live many years. But you must not lift anything, not even babies."

"But you can still hug them, Mother," said Ann Blaikie, International Link for the Co-Workers.

On June 19th, Mother asked for pen and paper to write the fruits of her meditation. "Who is Jesus to Me?" was the result of this prayer and meditation time while she was so close to death, and she shared it with her Sisters, Brothers, and Co-Workers. Her meditation ended, "Jesus, I love with my whole heart, with my whole being. I have given Him all, even my sins, and He has espoused me to Himself in tenderness and love. Now and for life, I am the spouse of my crucified Spouse. Amen."

On July 4th, Mother Teresa was released to Sister Gertrude, a medical doctor and the second woman to join the Missionaries of Charity.

Immediately after she left the hospital, Mother Teresa received a visit from Jozef Cardinal Glemp of Poland, who asked her to bring her Sisters to Warsaw. Sister Gertrude tried to convince Mother not to make a trip until she was stronger, but Mother was soon on her way to Poland.

In less than seven weeks, Mother Teresa was traveling across the Atlantic to the United States. In New York she visited with her friend Cardinal Cooke, who was dying of cancer. He had given her an empty convent for her new Priest Co-Worker Movement, called Corpus Christi. It consisted of priests from other orders such as Jesuit, Dominican and parish priests who volunteered to work with the Missionaries of Charity.

The Missionaries of Charity Brothers were now pretty well on their own, operating separately, and Mother felt the Priest Co-Workers would separate also.

When Mother returned for a checkup, her doctors were concerned. "Mother Teresa, you have to slow down. Take it easy. The way you live would kill a person much younger than you with a healthy heart. We almost lost you this summer. Won't you please cooperate?"

"I'm sorry, doctor," Mother said. "But I can feel Jesus calling me in the poorest of the poor and I have never said no to Him and I can't start now."

Mother told her Sisters that when she was almost comatose and it was too painful for her to say anything, she had a dream: "I knocked on the gates of heaven and St. Peter said, 'We're not ready for you, Mother Teresa. You are needed in the slums. There are no slums up here.'"

A Greater Vision

Things did not slow down for Mother Teresa.

In November 1983, only six months after she was put on medication for her weakening heart, Mother Teresa flew to Hong Kong to see her Sisters in the center they had opened earlier that year. While she was there, Mother received a message asking her to come to Delhi to meet with Queen Elizabeth II, who would award her with one of Britian's most prestigious honors, the Order of Merit.

A few months later, Mother Teresa received a call from Pope John Paul II, inviting her to speak at an international rally of Catholic youth to be held in Rome. In April of 1984, she addressed the young people in St. Peter's Square and later at the Coliseum, where Brother Roger of Taizé joined her.

While in Rome, Mother Teresa told Cardinal Cassaroli, the Vatican Secretary of State, "I want to offer the services of my Sisters to the people of China." For many years, Chinese bishops and priests who retained a link with Rome were persecuted, jailed and even killed. Chinese Catholics had to turn away from Rome and give their allegiance to the Chinese Patriotic Church in order to worship openly. Pope John Paul II was eager to establish ties with China's Patriotic Church and Mother Teresa hoped that she and the Missionaries of Charity could help accomplish this.

Prior to her talk with the Cardinal, Mother had visited the Chinese Embassy in New Delhi with the hopes the Missionaries of Charity could go to China. After the embassy official visited Nirmal Hriday, he offered to help her. Communist authorities told Mother that the Chinese government looked after their people so there were no poor there. "I am delighted to hear that you have no poor," she said, "but there may be some people who are despondent and need some encouragement. My Sisters and I would like to help." An official said, "We could allow your Sisters to do that much."

Mother wanted to make sure that a Roman Catholic priest went with her Sisters since Mother could not allow them to be without their sacraments. The Chinese felt Mother should accept a priest from the Chinese Patriotic Catholic Church. Mother, however, rejected this condition, since such a Chinese priest would not recognize the Pope.

So, instead of making the journey to China, she visited with Cardinal Josef Glemp in Poland at his invitation. She then returned to Rome and spent a few days in the hospital, where doctors told her once again she must slow down. Mother finally agreed that she must send other Sisters to travel the far reaches of the world in her place.

In October of that same year, Mother returned to Rome to address a world-wide retreat of priests. When she spoke to the 6,500 priests, her words were simultaneously translated into several languages since the priests came from every continent and represented every race of humanity.

All were inspired by the tiny woman who stood before them, sharing her complete love for Jesus, the One who gave her life meaning. As Mother spoke about the holiness of the priest in today's world, many priests were moved to tears. She said simply, "Be holy like Jesus."

After the Rome retreat, Father Joseph Langford, head of the Priest Co-Workers, approached Mother Teresa with an idea that had been in his mind for several years.

"Mother Teresa, many priests are inspired and sustained by your example. The Priest Co-Worker movement is growing rapidly. But some of us would like to make an even deeper commitment to your vision. I have spoken with many priests who would like to become a part of a congregation of priests related to the Missionaries of Charity."

"I've got a similar idea, Father," Mother Teresa said. "I have been praying about it for some time now."

The two of them went to the Sacred Congregation for the Doctrine of Faith and announced their idea for a congregation which would be called the Missionaries of Charity Fathers. Father Joseph Langford and three other priests were allowed to begin novitiate training in the Bronx.

"I don't think I'll start anything more," Mother Teresa told her Sisters. She was seventy-four years old and had just added yet another new society to her spiritual family.

On October 31, 1984, Mother's friend, Prime Minister Indira Gandhi, was assassinated by her Sikh bodyguards after the Indian military had stormed the Golden Temple, the sacred place of the Sikhs. Mother flew to India for the cremation on the banks of the Jumna River in New Delhi.

"May her soul live in peace forever," Mother prayed.

Mother Teresa and her Sisters visited Sikhs hiding out of fear of reprisal, some of whom had witnessed others of their religion killed.

"We must love one another," Mother told the Indian people. "That is all Jesus came to tell us."

In December 1984, poisonous gas escaped from a pesticide plant in Bhopal, India owned by a subsidiary of the U.S. corporation Union Carbide. Over 25,000 people died and many more were seriously harmed by the gas. Mother Teresa and her Sisters immediately flew to Bhopal. Mother told the angry mob she met at the airport, "God bless you. You have to forgive. Forgive." She then visited everyone in the hospital and said, "I am here to give love and care to those who need it most in this terrible tragedy."

On Christmas of 1984, Mother Teresa was on her way to Ethiopia, concerned about Africa's famine, which began when the Ethiopian economy, already disrupted by war, was crippled by a severe drought. Relief efforts were very difficult since the country was torn apart by civil war.

Mother had been told that it would be impossible for Christians to help the suffering in Ethiopia, but her iron will made the impossible possible once again. She brought food and medication from Calcutta, but soon realized that the need outweighed what she had by far. Emperor Haile Selassie's daughter, though, admired what Mother Teresa and her Missionaries of Charity did around the world, and arranged a meeting with the Minister of the Imperial Court for Mother. After interviewing Mother Teresa, the Minister asked her if she tried to convert people to Christianity.

Mother answered, "Our works of love reveal to the suffering poor the love of God for them."

She was then introduced to the emperor, who said, "I have heard about the good work you do. I am very happy you have come. Yes, let your Sisters come to Ethiopia."

"Ethiopia is an open Calvary," Mother Teresa said when she returned to visit her Sisters there in 1985. Eight teams of her Sisters were caring for the starving people, some of whom died in Mother's arms.

Bob Geldof, the rock singer from Dublin who led the "LiveAid" musicians in their successful campaign to raise $9,000,000 for the famine victims with the song "Do They Know It's Christmas" (and millions more with simultaneous concerts held on two continents in July 1985), wanted to meet with Mother.

She met with him and although they obviously came from radically different backgrounds, they realized that by pooling their efforts, they could make a difference.

"I was so impressed by how you approach government officials, Mother Teresa," Bob Geldof told her. "I couldn't believe it, the way you asked for and received an empty building for an orphanage."

"I just put everything in God's hands. It is His work and He arranges everything," Mother said.

Bob Geldof later said that "she was the living embodiment of moral good."

When she returned to Calcutta, Mother Teresa asked President Reagan for help. This resulted in aid reaching the villages that were cut off by government forces who confiscated the food for themselves.

1,000,000 people died of starvation during the Ethiopian famine, but 7,000,000 people threatened with death by starvation were saved by these massive efforts.

In January 1985 one of Mother Teresa's most fervent prayers was finally answered when the Patriotic Church invited her to visit China. She went to Beijing accompanied by Sister Dorothy, former regional superior of Japan, Hong Kong, Macao, Taiwan and South Korea.

During the four days they were there, the Chinese government treated them with great kindness. Mother Teresa usually stayed in a convent when she traveled, but since China had few nuns and no convents, she found herself in a luxury hotel.

The two nuns went to Mass at the Cathedral of the Immaculate Conception. The elderly priest said a Mass in beautiful Latin. After Mass, Mother had a long discussion with Deng Pufang, the son of Deng Xiaoping, China's Premier. The young man was in a wheelchair. Deng Pufang was deputy director of China's Welfare Fund for the Handicapped. He had broken his back when he was thrown out of a window by Red Guards during the Cultural Revolution. Deng Pufang praised Mother Teresa's work with the poorest people. As he described China's efforts to help the handicapped, he said, "Although we come from different standpoints, we are doing similar work."

Mother said, "It is the same standpoint, out of love for God in action."

"Regardless of the social system, we are doing the same thing for the same purpose," Deng said. "We both want to help our people. However, I myself am an atheist."

Mother continued, "The same loving hand has created you and me. What you do is your love for God in action. You put that desire into action and that is love."

Deng arranged for Mother Teresa to visit one of the 1,600 state workshop factories for the handicapped. Mother examined the work of over 200 factory workers, many of them blind, and she wrote, "God bless you all," in the visitor's book.

And she told the foreman, who was blind, "I will pray for you and all who work for you." He smiled.

"Pray for me," Mother Teresa said.

"We owe everything to the Communist Party," he replied.

After she visited one of the government collectives, Mother Teresa said, "Although the government has a very extensive welfare program, my Sisters could provide some tender love and care for those who need it most."

Asked if she had brought any message from the Vatican to the estranged Chinese Patriotic Catholic Association, she replied, "No, I'm coming from Calcutta."

When she was asked, "What is a Communist to you?" she said, "A child of God, my brother or sister."

As she did during her previous visit, Mother explained that a Roman Catholic priest would have to be available to the Sisters for their spiritual needs while in China. And, as before, Mother was offered a priest from the Chinese Patriotic Catholic Chuch. The impasse remained.

Mother Teresa was very disappointed that no agreement to open a home resulted from her visit, but despite this, she assured the government and the National Association of Patriotic Catholics that a team of Sisters would be ready to come to China any time they were wanted.

Mother's appearances with heads of countries, politicians and famous people, accepting awards and prizes made her a target of public opinion. She was often criticized for her high profile. But thanks to her high profile, over 100,000 school children in Denmark went without a glass of milk in order that others might eat; 800,000 capsules of Lampren have been sent annually from Switzerland to the lepers in west Bengal; 5,000 tons of high-quality processed food were dispatched at a week's notice for the famine-stricken people of Ethiopia and Tanzania—these missions were accomplished because of Mother Teresa's contact with the public. Her "poorest of the poor" were made known to the world, loved and cared for.

Mother Teresa passed her seventy-fifth birthday on August 26, 1985, at the Mother House in Calcutta. She was with her Sisters as they prayed in meditation and in serving the poor in the Home for the Dying, the Children's Home, medical clinics for the lepers, and slum schools.

Mother was making plans for the General Chapter of the Missionaries of Charity, a meeting held every six years. On September 22, 1985, she brought to the Mother House eight Sisters, representing Sisters all over the world, and fifteen regional Superiors and delegates elected from each region. In addition, there were six Councilors from Calcutta who helped conduct the business of the congregation. They began their meeting with a retreat in the small chapel of the Mother House.

On October 7th, the thirty-fifth anniversary of the founding of the Order, Mother Teresa was elected the Superior General and Sister Agnes was elected Assistant

General. The other Councilors were Sister Priscilla, Sister Shanti, Sister Camillus, Sister Dorothy and Sister Andrea. Their joint mission was to guide the Order until 1991.

To celebrate their fortieth anniversary, the United Nations invited Ann and Jeanette Petrie to show their documentary film, "The World of Mother Teresa," and on October 26, 1985, the United Nations Secretary General Xavier Perez de Cuellar introduced Mother Teresa.

"This is a hall of words," the Secretary General began. "A few days ago, we had on this rostrum the most powerful men in the world. Now we have the privilege to have the most powerful woman in the world. She is peace in the world."

Mother looked extremely small and stooped as she stood at the green marble podium from which presidents, prime ministers, foreign ministers, kings, sultans, and chancellors had spoken. She bowed and began, "1986 has been designated as the World Year of Peace. Let us say together the prayer for peace. Works of love are works of peace."

Just as she had done in Oslo before receiving the Nobel Peace Prize, she had St. Francis' Prayer for Peace passed out to every member of the audience at the United Nations.

"If we have the joy of seeing God in one another, we will love one another. That is why no color, no religion, no nationality should come between us, for we are all children of the same loving hand of God, created for greater things, to love and to be loved. We all want peace. We are frightened of nuclear war. We are frightened of this terrible new disease. But we are not frightened to kill an innocent child, the little unborn child who has been created for the same purpose, love."

The reporters asked her, "Mother Teresa, what do you have to say about the nuclear arms race?"

"I don't know much about that," she said, "But I do know that anything that destroys life is evil."

A reporter asked, "What do you think about a just war, Mother?"

She said, "War is killing human beings. How could this ever be just? How could war be just?"

"But your church teaches there can be a just war," the reporter said.

"I could never agree to the taking of a human life," Mother kept shaking her head.

"Catholics have to believe in the teaching about just war," the reporter insisted.

"Then I'm not a good Catholic?" Mother said.

When Mother spoke of a "terrible new disease" in her speech at the United Nations, she was speaking about AIDS (acquired immune deficiency syndrome). She heard there were many babies born with AIDS in New York City, so she went to speak with Mayor Koch about opening a home for children with the disease.

"Mother Teresa, I am so happy you want to open a house for children with AIDS," he said, "but do you realize that AIDS is the number one killer for young men in their thirties in New York City? Could you open a home for them, Mother?"

"Yes, Your Honor," Mother said. "We will open one as soon as we can make the arrangements."

On Christmas Eve of 1985, Mother opened her first home for AIDS patients in New York's Greenwich Village in the former rectory of St. Veronica's Church. She named it "Gift of Love." "AIDS is so much like leprosy," Mother said. "I never thought I would open a home for the dying in New York City." Four Sisters worked in this house devoting their lives to the fourteen or fifteen men who came there to die with AIDS.

The first to die in the house was Harvey, a Vietnam War veteran with a history of drugs. Before he died he said, "Sister, could you please bring the priest to baptize me?" The priest came right away, baptized him and gave him the Last Rites. The Sisters were overjoyed. "Do you want to go to heaven?" one of them asked him.

"Oh, yes," he said. "But I don't want to leave this house. It is so full of love and peace here."

"All of the love and all of the peace you find here comes from Jesus and you will see Him face to face in heaven," the Sisters told him.

"Sisters," he asked, "would you help me?"

"Of course. What can we do for you?"

"Teach me to pray. I want to talk to God."

They taught him the Lord's Prayer. One Sister said, "Just talk to God the way you would talk to your own father."

"And don't forget to listen to His answers," another Sister said. "Mother Teresa says that prayer begins with silence. God speaks to our heart in the silence. And then we can talk to God from our heart and He will listen."

One of the Sisters brought the Bible. "Mother also says that prayer begins with Scripture. We listen to God speaking in the Bible and then we speak to Him from our heart and He listens. That is prayer."

They read him the 32nd Psalm:

How blessed is he whose transgression is forgiven, whose sin is covered!

How blessed is the man to whom the Lord does not impute iniquity,
And in whose spirit there is no deceit!
When I kept silent about my sin, my body wasted away
Through my groaning all day long.
For day and night Thy hand was heavy upon me;
My vitality was drained away as with the fever heat of summer.
Selah. I acknowledged my sin to Thee,
And my iniquity I did not hide;
I said, "I will confess my transgressions to the Lord,"
And Thou didst forgive the guilt of my sin.
Selah. Therefore, let everyone who is godly pray to Thee in a time when Thou mayest be found;
Surely in a flood of great waters they shall not reach him.
Thou art my hiding place;
Thou dost preserve me from trouble;
Thou dost surround me with songs of deliverance.
Selah. I will instruct you and teach you in the way which you should go;
I will counsel you with My eye upon you.
Do not be as the horse or as the mule which have no understanding, whose trappings include bit and bridle to hold them in check.
Otherwise they will not come near to you.
Many are the sorrows of the wicked;
But he who trusts in the Lord, loving kindness shall surround him.
Be glad in the Lord and rejoice, you righteous ones, and shout for joy all you who are upright in heart.

When they finished the Psalm, Harvey smiled and closed his eyes forever. He died peacefully as did most of the people fortunate enough to die in the loving care of Mother and her Missionaries of Charity.

Whenever Pope John Paul II traveled, there were certain rituals he followed. The first time he landed in a country, he got down on his knees and kissed the ground. And every time he landed anywhere, his first stop was the nearest chapel for prayer and the Cathedral, if there was one nearby, for Mass. However, in February 1986, when the Pope landed in Calcutta, he asked to be taken directly to Mother Teresa's Home for the Dying.

He quoted Gandhi: "Conquer hate by love, untruth by truth, violence by suffering," as he went with Mother Teresa from cot to cot, bending down to touch each one of the dying, helping to feed some of the weakest. He said something to each one of the patients.

"Come and see us again," one little Hindu woman said.

The Pope went into the little morgue with Mother and blessed the four men who had died earlier that day. When he was preparing to leave, Mother Teresa said, "Thank you, Holy Father, for blessing us with your visit."

"Thank you, Mother Teresa, for reminding us that God is in love with each one of us and never stops trying to win our love."

After the Holy Father left, Mother Teresa said, "I have had many happy days, but this is the happiest day of my life."

Eight Days and Nights

Mother Teresa continued to dream of seeking out the poor, the sick and the dying all around the world. Despite the fact that she was increasingly frail and sickly, she was still active, going, for example, to the India-Nepal border region in August of 1988 to help victims of an earthquake, and then on to racially segregated South Africa a few months later.

That same year, a delegation of bishops who went to China to seek the reunion of Chinese Catholics reported to Mother that she and her Sisters would be welcome there on two conditions: the work must be social, not spiritual or religious, and the Sisters could not wear the sari but must dress in the Chinese style. Mother was agreeable to these conditions and was hopeful that a home could finally be established there. She asked that special prayers be said for the fulfillment of her dream.

Her prayer to St. Joseph for a home in South Africa was answered when she founded a convent for her nuns in Khayelitsha, a black township outside of Cape Town. Although she was accused of making her mission political, she made it clear that the invitation had come from Roman Catholic Archbishop George Daniel. "I did not know that Apartheid or something like it existed," she said. "White, black, green, yellow, whatever, you are all children of God, created for greater things, to love and be loved." Mother left South Africa in November 1988 with plans to return and open a second house in the Winterveld area.

In early September 1989, Mother became critically ill. When her vomiting and high fever would not stop, she was taken to Woodland Nursing Home in Calcutta. She remained in intensive care, watched over by her Italian doctor and an American doctor. They told her Sisters, "Mother Teresa has angina pectoris. Two of her arteries are completely blocked and she must have a pacemaker."

The world prayed for her and get-well wishes arrived from the President of India as well as many other heads of state. The doctors implanted the pacemaker and Mother recovered enough to continue her mission. The world breathed a sigh of relief.

In late 1989, the people of Communist East Germany began dismantling the Berlin Wall. Erected in 1961 to discourage the flood of refugees from seeking freedom in the West, it symbolized tyranny, the "iron curtain." When it came down, the world rejoiced. In the footsteps of this monumental event, citizens of Hungary, Romania and other repressed countries rose against their Communist leaders, who had controlled them for years.

In spite of her ill health, Mother acted right away. She went to the countries whose religious needs were most pressing. Five houses were opened in the USSR and one in Armenia. Surviving on the strength of her prayers, she went on to establish a children's home in Bucharest for young AIDS victims and two homes in Czechoslovakia.

More and more, poor health and advanced age limited Mother's activities. During Holy Week 1990, she asked Pope John Paul II to let her resign as head of her order. He accepted her request and a General Chapter was convened in Calcutta to elect her successor. Many of her Sisters wanted Mother to stay in office until she died; others felt she should step down to train a successor while continuing as their spiritual advisor.

Behind these chaotic scenes, something interesting was unfolding. A few days before the election, Sister Agnes, the First Councillor of the Active Branch, and Sister Nirmala, head of the Contemplative Branch, went to Father Van Exem, who was confined to his sickbed.

They asked, "Father, may the Sisters re-elect Mother?"

Father Van Exem smiled and replied, "There is nothing in church law to prevent such a thing."

Worldwide, the media frenzy escalated. Who would take over for Mother? Twelve miles outside of Calcutta, at Dum Dum, an unsuspecting Mother and her Sisters met. Strong iron gates prevented the media from entering the compound. Eight days and nights of prayer and silence preceded the election. When the results were announced, Mother was proclaimed the winner. The media around the world was shocked but her Sisters rejoiced—they so dearly wanted Mother to remain Superior General of her beloved Missionaries of Charity. Apparently, God was not ready to relinquish Mother's special magic which opened the hearts of reluctant leaders all around the world.

Mother had wanted to resign and to train a replacement, but the Sisters had insisted on keeping her as their official head. With the celebration of her eightieth birthday just days beforehand, Mother Teresa accepted her re-election as the will of God.

"I had expected to be free," Mother admitted, "but God has His own plans."

Mother Teresa told her Sisters, "Believe me, my dear children, pay close attention to what Mother is saying now—only the thirst of Jesus, hearing it, feeling it, answering it with all your heart will keep the Society alive after Mother leaves you. Jesus' thirst will never leave you. Jesus thirsting in the poor you will have with you always. Let Our Lady bring you face to face with the love in the heart of Jesus crucified. Hear Him. Hear your own name. Make my joy and yours complete."

As she lay in hospital beds more and more frequently, somehow keeping death at bay, Mother kept her dearest dreams alive—to open a Missionaries of Charity house in China and to open another in her homeland, Albania, where her mother and sister were buried.

Albania was the last stronghold of Communism in Eastern Europe. In the spring of 1990, their Communist regime was on the defensive. Mother had approached government officials and said, "I want to open a house here."

They told her, "Mother, to open a Missionaries of Charity home would be to break the law."

"Then I will break the law," Mother said. Breaking the law wasn't necessary, though, since the twenty-year-old ban on religion was soon lifted. The citizens were finally allowed to practice their religion without punishment. The new head of Albania, Ramiz Alia, welcomed Mother and congratulated her on her selfless work. He said, "The world calls you Mother Teresa of Calcutta. But we call you Mother Teresa of Albania."

An Albanian priest accompanied Mother and the first four Sisters to open the new home for the aged. Mother said, "We will begin slowly and see what is the greatest need." Soon she had four houses in Albania.

Having demonstrated time and time again that no country was too far away, no danger too frightening for Mother and her Missionaries of Charity, she was soon off to Romania, appearing on Romanian television.

In August of 1990 Iraq invaded Kuwait. The United Nations demanded a complete withdrawal of all Iraqi forces, but Iraq's leader, Saddam Hussein, showed no signs of budging. President George Bush of the United States threatened to retaliate if Iraq didn't free Kuwait, from which the U.S. imported a large amount of oil. Concerned about the threat of war, Mother wrote a joint letter to both Bush and Hussein. "I come to you with tears in my eyes and God's love in my heart," she said. "I plead to you for those who will be left orphaned, widowed, and left alone because their parents, husbands, brothers and children have been killed. I beg you to save them . . . Please choose the way of peace."

Both heads of state ignored Mother's pleas, and the United States and its allies sent over 600,000 troops for a massive air attack on Iraq. Saddam Hussein's troops were defeated in a mere four days. An official cease-fire was accepted and signed on April 6, 1991.

When Mother arrived in Baghdad at the invitation of Saddam Hussein, she found terrible destruction. She opened a home for the elderly, and on the grounds of the convent of the Dominican Presentation a house was made ready and soon filled with children crippled and suffering from malnutrition.

In late 1991, Mother Teresa went to Tijuana, Mexico, the fastest growing border town in the world. "I have never seen worse poverty," she remarked. After visiting the Missionaries of Charity soup kitchen, the home for the elderly and the convent, she went to the Seminary to attend the Ordination Mass of a Missionaries of Charity Brother.

Mother celebrated the Feast of Our Lady of Guadalupe in Tijuana on December 12. Shortly after that, she had a critical heart attack and was transferred to Scripps Hospital in La Jolla, California, near San Diego. She was cared for by the country's top specialists.

Again the world prayed for Mother's survival. Concerned for her health, the Holy Father called her several times. Once, Bishop Brom was visiting Mother when Pope John Paul II called. Mother was near death at the time, so the Bishop took the call. He handed the phone to Mother Teresa. Her weakened arm shook as she held it. She listened a minute, then put the receiver on her bed and said, "He said he loves me." She picked up the phone and said, "Holy Father, I love you too. And I love the whole world." No one in the room had dry eyes.

Shortly afterward, in early 1992, Mother Teresa begged her doctors to let her return to Calcutta. When she stopped in Rome en route, she became ill again and was admitted to the hospital.

Someone asked, "Mother, are you afraid of death?"

She said, "Oh, no! I see it every day. Death is the shortest way to God. It's the way home."

Mother had planned to meet Diana, Princess of Wales, in Calcutta. When Diana arrived at the Mother House, she learned Mother was ill in Rome. Nonetheless, Diana went to Nirmal Hriday, the home for the dying. Unafraid and with loving spirit, Diana touched the bodies of the suffering, showing them compassion before they went home to God. In return, she received their smiles.

Mother's eighty-third birthday was spent in the All-India Institute of Medical Science Hospital in New Delhi. She was plagued with fever and vomiting. Suffering from congestion of the lungs, once more her heart became cause for serious concern. But, predictably, the next day she boarded a plane and returned to Calcutta. By September 17th, however, Mother Teresa was once more fighting for her life. This time surgeons attempted to clear a blocked heart vessel. While she was in intensive care, Father Celeste Van Exem, her spiritual director, died at St. Xavier's College, Calcutta. Shortly before his death, he wrote a letter to Mother telling her that he was offering his life that she might return to China.

Having beaten death yet again, Mother finally did return to China in 1993 and again in March of 1994. Both times Mother met with Deng Pufang in hopes that the Missionaries of Charity Sisters be allowed to bring love and care to the poor. But the dream that was closest to her heart was again denied, in part, at least, because of the continued lack of agreement on spiritual allegiance. Until her death, though, Mother never gave up trying to open a home in China. "China, it seems, needed more prayers."

In April 1996, Mother fell and broke her collarbone. In June she broke her foot but kept traveling in a wheelchair. Somehow, she managed to open her 565th house, in Wales. By the end of August she was again in intensive care at Woodland's Nursing Home in Calcutta and could only breathe with the assistance of a respirator. On the eve of her eighty-sixth birthday, to the amazement of her doctors, Mother was able to breathe without the respirator, and by September 6th she insisted she felt well enough to be released. But by the 25th she was back in the hospital where a scan revealed a shadow on the brain. Many rumors of her death circulated, but on December 19, 1996 Mother miraculously walked out of the hospital and returned to the Mother House, where she was confined to bed with severe back pain.

In January of 1997 Archbishop Henry D'Souza of Calcutta announced that Mother Teresa had made it clear she wished to resign as Superior General of her order. Her health simply would not allow her to continue.

Once more the Missionaries of Charity cloistered themselves and spent eight days and nights in silent prayer before the election of Mother's successor. On March 13, 1997, the Missionaries of Charity chose Sister Nirmala, former head of the Contemplative Sisters. Pope John Paul II suggested that Mother remain spiritual head and help the newly-elected Superior General, which she did.

Most people expected Mother's replacement to come from the Active Branch, but Mother Teresa had always said, "We can't do our physical works of mercy unless we spend time in meditation, listening to the Lord." She once again thought of St. Thérèse of Lisieux, who offered her daily prayers and sufferings for the missions.

Mother Teresa continued to receive prestigious awards. On June 5, 1997, she received the Congressional Medal in Washington D.C. for "outstanding and enduring contributions to humanity and charitable works."

During this visit, Mother Teresa met Princess Diana for the last time at Mother's convent in the South Bronx. The Princess was in New York to visit AIDS patients and to meet friends. When a Co-Worker announced her arrival, Mother said, "I'm busy right now." She never raised her head but continued to wash the human skeleton lying on the thin mattress. "Show the Princess what she can do to be helpful."

Princess Diana made her way down the rows of suffering bodies. Her infectious smile comforted the dying; words of encouragement gave hope to the lonely, and her hands administered to the sick. This lasting application of love and compassion were the qualities that endeared Diana to Mother Teresa.

Little did the world know that both would be gone before the summer was over.

Safely Home

On the morning of September 3, 1997, Mother asked her old friend, Michael Gomes (who still lived at 14 Creek Lane) to take her to the graveyard of St. John's Church where one of her Missionaries of Charity was buried. The next day they went again. This was the graveyard for the religious where Mother expected to be buried. Perhaps she had a premonition of what was about to happen.

The rains were coming down the night of September 5th. Mother Teresa was in her room, writing letters, planning to attend a memorial service at St. Paul's Cathedral in Calcutta for Princess Diana, who had been killed in an automobile accident in Paris only a few days before.

During that evening, Mother Teresa dictated her final letter to the Missionaries of Charity and Co-Workers.

At 9:00 p.m., when Mother was getting ready for evening prayers, she had a bad pain in her chest. She fell on her mat and passed out. Sister Nirmala called the doctor who was nearby. He was there when Mother came to, put her arm to her chest and said, "I can't breathe." Several of the nuns heard Mother say, "Jesus, I love you," which was something she said constantly, aloud and to herself with every breath. In moments, Mother Teresa was gone from this world. All the Sisters rushed to Mother's room and hugged her and cried. By midnight the convent was surrounded by people who had come to mourn Calcutta's own saint.

Mother's body was embalmed and wrapped in an Indian flag over her sari. She was taken to St. Thomas' Church in Middleton Row, Calcutta in a Missionaries of Charity ambulance, and put on view. Her feet were bare. The rains continued as fifty thousand people came each day to say good-bye.

The Indian government insisted on giving Mother a state funeral similar to the one they had given to Gandhi. The same gun carriage that had carried Gandhi's body was used.

Sister Nirmala made sure that half of the 15,000 seats in the Netahu Indoor Stadium, the site of the funeral, were reserved for the lepers, the orphans, and the poor that the Missionaries of Charity had cared for.

Pope John Paul II, advancing in age and in poor health, was not in attendance. Cardinal A. Sadano, who represented the Pope, read his message: "She is a woman who has left her mark on history of this century. She was a glowing example of how the love of God can be transformed to the love of one's neighbor. Dear Mother

Teresa, rest in peace. Dear Mother Teresa, pray for all."

Mother Teresa and Princess Diana were two of the most famous women in the world in the 20th century. They had much love and respect for each other. That they should die the same week stunned the world. The ongoing news coverage of Diana's death, however, totally overshadowed that of Mother Teresa's. It was as though Princess Diana's spirit was saying to Mother Teresa's, "I have died first, still young, with some mystery surrounding my death, and you, who have given so much, can slip into heaven unnoticed."

Mother Teresa's final resting place is a simple room in the Calcutta Mother House where she lived and carried out her life's work.

The universe echoes Mother Teresa's words of comfort: "They are with the Father. They're safely home."

Epilogue

Every century or two, when darkness threatens humanity, God sends a holy person to light our way, a special messenger reminding the world of His unconditional love and His longing for humankind to love Him in one another. Those who shared the earth with Mother Teresa were blessed in many ways. She inspired many with her great compassion, her enormous love for the poor, the leper, the condemned killer, the dying.

Mother Teresa was the conscience of the world. She was the symbol of love, faithfulness, goodness and caring. Just knowing she was in the world gave many a feeling of security. A Biblical story tells how a prophet asked God if He would save the world if He could find ten good men in it and God said, "I will spare the world if I can find one." As long as Mother Teresa was in our world, it could be said that God could find at least one good soul.

Mother has been gone for a while now and the world is just beginning to recognize the greatness of its loss.

Brother Angelo Devananda, who helped Mother start a contemplative order of the Missionaries of Charity Brothers, said, "When the time comes for Mother to leave us . . . it will be the real heart and spiritual vision of her life that will endure and shine brightly as a light in the midst of the uncertainty of our world. Mother is like the true teacher whose desire is to point beyond, and then to disappear."

But in a deeper sense Mother is still here. Mother's patron saint, the Little Flower, St. Thérèse of Lisieux, promised on her deathbed, "I will spend my Heaven doing good for those on earth." Jesus said, "Know that I am with you always until the end of the world." Mother Teresa, who followed Jesus and St. Thérèse so closely, will surely do the same.

In the Middle Ages, when a very holy person died, the local church had the right to canonize them. St. Francis of Assisi, who like Mother Teresa chose to live in poverty and care for lepers and the poor, was canonized only two years after his death.

Cardinal Roger Mahoney of Los Angeles wrote to Pope Paul II, asking him to waive the five year delay. Cardinal Joseph Ratzinger, the Vatican's top doctrinal official, said, "Because her life was so resplendent before the eyes of everybody, her cause will not present many problems so I don't think too long a process will be necessary."

The Pope has agreed to speed up the process. He has waived the five year wait before beginning and promised to do what he could to expedite the process. Since the Holy Father and Mother Teresa were such close friends, he is well aware of her holiness. "She will be a saint," he promised.

Twelve investigators began studying Mother's life on July 26, 1999. After the investigation is completed, she will be declared venerable if the investigators are satisfied that she led an exemplary life. Next, a miracle is required, probably a healing that doctors declare miraculous, after which Mother Teresa would be beatified and called Blessed. Then, after another miracle which happens after she is beatified, she would be canonized, which means the Church declares that she is with God and her life is an example for us.

Information about many "miracles" is being sent to the Vatican for consideration.

Mother Teresa's legacy of love inspires her Missionaries of Charity Sisters, Brothers, Priests, and her Co-Workers to continue helping the world's impoverished people. She left over 4,500 nuns in 585 houses in over 120 countries. Her personal touch and her global vision has inspired all who have helped her carry on the work.

When people asked Mother what would happen to her order once she died, she said, "God will find someone who will do the work. I'm only an instrument in God's hands. It is His work. He will see that it continues."

In her letter dated November 24, 1998 from her retreat in Monsada near the border of Bangladesh, Sister Nirmala wrote these words to her Co-Workers, both Active and Sick and Suffering: "Please pray for me and for all our Sisters, especially the ninety-five who will make their first vows and seventy-seven who will make their final vows in different parts of the world this December. You will be very happy to know that since Mother's going home to Jesus, we have been able to offer Jesus twenty new Tabernacles all around the world, and after the profession in December, we are offering Him another fifteen new Tabernacles."

Rev. Camille Bouche, a Calcutta priest for fifty years and spiritual father to the Missionaries of Charity novices, says, "In the near term people will continue to give, but after two or three years it will depend on how the new leaders use their money. If they keep on looking after the poor, they will be all right. The flow of dollars will slow down but it will continue."

There is no question that at the speed with which the Missionaries of Charity Order and Tabernacles are growing, the world can expect their survival and that their work caring for abandoned babies, the dying, the lepers, the people with AIDS, will continue. The Sisters bring God's love and joy to all of them. The Co-

Workers get together once a month for prayer, adoration of the Blessed Sacrament, or Mass, then gather to share the immediate problems in the neighborhood and what they can do. They may work with the Missionaries of Charity in their soup kitchens, orphanages, or hospices. They visit AIDS patients, gather blankets for homeless, have parties for poor and sick children.

One reason Mother's Missionaries of Charity have few problems continuing without her is the fact that the various international homes ran on their own even while Mother was alive. Mother was only able to visit many of the homes a few times, so they were already used to operating without her physical presence.

The Holy Father began the year 2000 with what he called a "Vatican Woodstock." He invited children from all over the world and sponsored a concert right outside his window. He invited Sister Nirmala to come and speak to them. Their warm relationship with the Holy Father is one reason the Missionaries of Charity have continued to thrive.

Sister Nirmala has said, "We are determined the work will go on. We, Mother's Sisters, know the best tribute we can give to her is continuing what she taught us with her life and her example, wherever we are." She ends her talks with, "Please pray for us as we continue the work with our most needful and as we speak the Gospel of Love."

When some people wanted to call her Mother now that she is the head of the order, Sister Nirmala said, "No, Mother Teresa is our Mother."

One problem facing Mother's order is the fact that many Christians are being tortured for their faith today. Father A.T. Thomas, a Jesuit priest, was beheaded in Bihar, India on October 28, 1997. Not long afterwards highway robbers, reported to be religious fanatics, stole a truck carrying food and medicine from Calcutta to Mother Teresa's home in Patna. They killed Missionaries of Charity Brother Luke Puttaniyil and the two volunteers who were in the truck with him.

In January of 1998, Missionaries of Charity Sisters were held hostage in Freetown, Sierra Leone. Three were shot and killed. Four were released, including the wounded Sister Indu, an Xaverian Missionary Brother, and two other hostages. Sister Indu died one week after being released. Three more Sisters were shot and died in Hodieda, Yemen in July of 1998 by a man suspected of being an extremist while leaving their convent on their way to work in their soup kitchen.

In her November 1998 letter to the Co-Workers, Sister Nirmala wrote: "Our seven Sisters went home to Jesus in little over one month this year. Mother seems to be gathering many more intercessors around her to pray for all of us. Let us pray for them and ask them to pray for us."

Mother Teresa surrendered her life to her God and became "a pencil in His hands so He could write His love letter to the world." Today, that letter is still being written, in the form of Mother Teresa's Co-Workers and Missionaries, who affect the lives of over 4,000,000 people. What began as one tiny nun's relationship with Jesus has spread all over the world.

To her all life was precious. She would have given her own life to save an unborn baby or a convicted serial killer condemned to capital punishment. She saw Jesus in everyone. She felt the whole world's pain, heard the afflicted crying in the night and rushed to comfort them.

Once she met Jesus, she never took her eyes off Him. He wasn't, as Mother often said, always easy to please but He kept His promises and she could count on Him to fill her life with miracles when she needed them most.

By being God's instrument of love, peace and healing, she showed the world what one human being can do, how one can work through God, with whom all things are possible.

"We are all called to love," Mother Teresa said, and the example of her life reminds us that the future of humanity depends on whether we are listening.

Mother Teresa, by Millie Crawford

Index

Bibliography

Accurso, Lina. "What Mother Teresa Means to Me," *Liguorian*, p. 17, February 1983.

Bang, Kirsten. *Yougga Finds Mother Teresa*, Element Books, Tisbury, Wiltshire, 1983. (Translated by Kathryn Spink).

Bethell, Tom. "Mother Teresa's Sisters Help AIDS Victims," *Catholic Digest*, p. 36., January 1987, *The American Spectator*, 1986.

Chetcuti, S.J., Paul. *Choosing to Serve the Destitute*, Irish Messenger Publications, 1980. (Translated by Michael P. Gallagher, S.J.)

A. M. Cocagnac & Rosemary Haughton (ed.), *Bible for Young Christians*, The MacMillan Co., New York, 1966.

Constant, Audrey. *In the Streets of Calcutta, The Story of Mother Teresa*, Pergamon Press, London, 1980.

The Co-Worker Newsletter, Co-Workers of Mother Teresa in the United States, Vi Collins and Marge Murray (ed.). Bethesda, Maryland.

Craig, Mary. *Mother Teresa*, Hamilton Children's Books, London, 1983.

Day, Dorothy. *Thérèse*, Templegate Publishers, Springfield, Illinois, 1979.

Doig, Desmond. *Mother Teresa, Her People and Her Work,* Harper & Row, San Francisco, California, 1976.

Eagan, Eileen. "Mother Teresa, The Myth and the Person," *America*, March 22, 1980.

Eagan, Eileen. "Mother Teresa," *Saints are Now*, John J. Delaney (ed.), Image Books, Garden City, New York, 1983.

Eagan, Eileen. *Such A Vision of the Streets*, Doubleday & Co., Garden City, New York, 1986.

Fisher, Louis. *The Life of Mahatma Gandhi*, Harper & Row, New York, New York 1950.

Gasnick, Roy M., O.F.M. *The Francis Book*, Macmillan Publishing Co., Inc., New York, 1980.

Gasnick, Roy M., O.F.M. "The World's Most Popular Saint," *Catholic Digest*, p. 57, November 1982.

Gasnick, Ray M., O.F.M. *Mother Teresa of Calcutta*, Marvel Comics, New York City, 1984.

Ghezzi, Bert. "Mother Teresa's Contemplative Brothers," *Catholic Digest,* p. 1, September 1986.

Gjergji, Lush. *Mother Teresa, Her Life, Her Works*, New York City Press, New York 1991.

Gonzalez-Balado, Jose Luis. *Mother Teresa, Always the Poor,* Liguori Publications, Liguori, Missouri, 1980. (Adapted from *Madre Teresa de los Pobres.*)

Gonzalez-Balado, Jose Luis. *Stories of Mother Teresa, Her Smile and Her Words*, Liguori Publications, Liguori, Missouri, 1983. (Adapted from *La Sonrisa de los Pobres.*)

Goodwin, Jan. "A Week with Mother Teresa," *Ladies Home Journal*, May 1984.

Gorrée, Georges and Jean Barbier. *Love Without Boundaries, Mother Teresa of Calcutta*, Our Sunday Visitor, Inc., Huntington, Indiana, 1974. (Translated from *Amour sans Frontiere.*)

Hanley, Boniface, O.F.M. *Ten Christians*, Ave Maria Press, Notre Dame, Indiana, 1970.

Hendriz, Kathleen. "Mother Teresa's Brothers in L.A.," *Catholic Digest*, July 1977.

Hess, Rev. Robert S.C.J. *Passageway to Heaven, A Pilgrim's Diary*, Sacred Heart League, Walls, Mississippi, 1987.

Hobden, Sheila. *Mother Teresa, People With a Purpose*, SCM Press LTD., London, 1973.

I Thirst, International Link Letter for Youth Co-Workers of Mother Teresa, Malta.

International Associations of Co-Workers of Mother Teresa Newsletter, March 1983, Number 45.

Kaufman, Michael. "People . . . Mother Teresa," *San Francisco Chronicle*, December 10, 1979.

Kennedy, Terry. "Brother Anthony Joins Mother Teresa," *Catholic Digest*, p. 47, August 1986.

LaPierre, Dominique. *The City of Joy*, Warner Books, New York, 1985. (Translated from the French by Kathryn Spink.)

Lee, Betsy. *Mother Teresa, Caring for All God's Children*, Dillon Press, Minneapolis, Minnesota, 1981.

Le Joly, Edward. *Servant of Love, Mother Teresa and Her Missionaries of Charity*, Harper & Row, San Francisco, California, 1977.

Le Joly, Edward. *Mother Teresa, A Woman in Love*, Ave Maria Press, Notre Dame, Indiana, 1993.

Le Joly, Edward. *Mother Teresa of Calcutta, a Biography,* Dillon Press, Minneapolis, Minnesota, 1981.

Long, John C. "The Hands of Mother Teresa," *Catholic Digest*, p. 24, October 1982.

Marchand, Roger. *Mother Teresa of Calcutta, Her Life and Her Work*, Liguori Publications, Liguori, Missouri, 1982.

McBride, Alfred O. PRAEM. "Little Sisters Exalt Human Value," *The Catholic Times*, p. 9, Columbus, Ohio, July 1, 1983.

McGovern, James. *To Give the Love of Christ*, NY Emmaus Books, Paulist Press, 1978.

Mohan, Claire Jordan. *Mother Teresa's Someday,* Young Sparrow Press, Worchester, Pennsylvania, 1989.

"Mother Teresa of Calcutta," From Press Pack at the opening of Missionaries of Charity House in San Francisco, 1982.

"Mother Teresa Speaking at National Presbyterian Church," Co-Workers of Mother Teresa in America Inc., Washington D.C., 1974. (Audio Cassette)

"Mother Teresa Speaking at National Shrine of the Immaculate Conception in Washington, D.C. and at Notre Dame University, Baltimore, Maryland, Rochester, Minnesota," Co-Workers of Mother Teresa in America Inc., Washington D.C., 1975 (Audio Cassette)

Mother Teresa. *A Gift for God, Prayers and Meditations*, Harper & Row, New York, 1975.

Mother Teresa. *Heart of Joy*, Servant Books, Ann Arbor, Michigan, 1987.

Mother Teresa. *Jesus, the Word to be Spoken,* (Compiled by Brother Angelo Devanda Scolozzi), Servant Books, Ann Arbor, Michigan, 1986.

Mother Teresa. *Life in the Spirit, Reflections, Meditations and Prayers*, Harper & Row, San Francisco, California, 1983.

Mother Teresa. *Love: A Fruit Always in Season, Daily Meditations by Mother Teresa*, Dorothy S. Hunt (editor), Ignatius Press, San Francisco, California, 1987.

Mother Teresa. *Loving Jesus*, Jose Luis Gonzalez-Balado (editor), Servant Publications, Ann Arbor, Michigan, 1991.

Mother Teresa and Brother Roger of Taizé. *Meditations on the Way of the Cross*, The Pilgrim Press, New York, 1987.

Mother Teresa. *My Life for the Poor,* Ballantine Books, New York, 1987.

Mother Teresa. *One Heart Full of Love*, Jose Luis Gonzalez-Balado (editor), Servant Publications, Ann Arbor, Michigan, 1991.

Mother Teresa. *Praytimes with Mother Teresa, a New Adventure in Prayer* (Prepared by Eileen Egan and Kathleen Eagan, O.S.B.)

Mother Teresa. *Total Surrender*, Brother Angelo Devananda Scolozzi (editor), Servant Publications, Ann Arbor, Michigan, 1985.

Mother Teresa. "Woman and the Eucharist, 41st Eucharist Congress, Congress Cassettes," Ann Arbor, Michigan, 1976. (Audio Cassette)

Mother Teresa. "Our Ministry to the Poor, God's Expectation for Us," Talk given at the University of San Diego, 1988. (Audio Cassette)

Mother Teresa. *Words to Love By*, Ave Maria Press, Notre Dame, Indiana, 1983.

Mother Teresa. "Joy," *Family Circle*, p. 61, April 1, 1980.

Mother Teresa. "A Christmas Message," *Good Housekeeping*, p. 145, December 1983.

"Mother Teresa, Indian Nun Wins Nobel Peace Prize," *Los Angeles Times*, October 18, 1979.

Muggeridge, Malcolm. *Something Beautiful for God, Mother Teresa of Calcutta*, Harper & Row, New York, 1971.

Newsletter from Archdiocese of San Francisco "From Mother Teresa," Spring 1982.

Petrie, Ann. "The World of Mother Teresa," Ann Petrie Productions, 1985. (Movie).

Pogash, Carol. "In San Francisco, a Friend Sees Her as Christ Incarnate," *San Francisco Examiner*, p. 22, October 17, 1979.

Popson, Martha. *That We Might Have Life*, Doubleday & Co. Inc., New York, 1981.

Porter, David. *Mother Teresa, The Early Years*, William B. Eerdmans Publishing Co., Grand Rapids, Michigan, 1986.

Prial, Frank. "Calcutta Nun Awarded Nobel Peace Prize," *New York Times*, October 18, 1979.

Rae, Daphne. *Love Until it Hurts*, Harper & Row, San Francisco, California, 1981.

Reed, Edward (ed.). *Pacem in Terris*, Pocket Books, New York, 1965.

Rodriquez, Robert D. "St. Thérèse, the Little Way and Mary," *Catholic Digest*, p. 61, November 1982.

The San Diego Union-Tribune, September 6, 1997.

Scolozzi, Brother Angelo Devananda. *Mother Teresa, Contemplative in the Heart of the World*, Servant Books, Ann Arbor, Michigan, 1986.

Sebba, Anne. *Mother Teresa*, Julia MacRae Books, Franklin Watts Ltd., London, 1982.

Serrou, Robert. *Teresa of Calcutta*, McGraw Hill Book Co., New York City, 1980.

Spink, Kathryn. *The Miracle of Love*, Harper & Row, San Francisco, California, 1981.

Spink, Kathryn. *I Need Souls Like You*, Harper & Row, San Francisco, California, 1984.

Spink, Kathryn. *Mother Teresa: A Complete Authorized Biography,* Harper, San Francisco, 1997.

Spink, Kathryn. *Mother Teresa of Calcutta*, 1985 Calendar, Damer Press, London, 1984.

Srinivasa, Murthy B. *Mother Teresa and India*, Long Beach Publications, Long, Beach, California, 1983.

Sroka, Bill. "Mother Teresa's India," *Catholic Digest*, October 1980.

St. Teresa of Avila. *The Autobiography of St. Teresa of Avila*, Doubleday Press, London, 1984.

St. Thérèse of Lisieux, *The Autobiography of a Soul*, Doubleday Books, Garden City, New York, 1957. (Translated by John Beevers.)

Suarez, Federico. *Our Lady, the Virgin*, Scepter Publishers, Ltd., Dublin, Ireland, 1968. (Translated from *La Virgen, Nuestra Senora*.)

Tanghe, Omer. *For the Least of My Brothers, the Spirituality of Mother Teresa and Catherine Doherty,* Alba House, New York, 1989. (Translated from the Flemish by Jean MacDonald.)

Tower, Courtney. "Mother Teresa's Work of Grace," *Reader's Digest Special Feature*, p. 285, January 1988.

Ward, Barbara. *World Poverty—Can it be solved?* Franciscan Herald Press, Chicago, Illinois, 1966.

Vardey, Lucinda. *Mother Teresa, A Simple Path,* Ballantine Books, New York, 1995.

Watson, Jeanene D. *Teresa of Calcutta, Serving the Poorest of the Poor*, Mott Media, Milford, Illinois, 1984.